goats eat cans

volume 3

STEVEN NOVAK

-Steven Novak-

Published in the United States of America by Quiet Corner Press in cooperation with The Literary Underground, California.
www.litunderground.com

Copyright © 2013

All rights reserved. No part of this publication may be reproduced or transmitted in any form or by any means, electronic or mechanical, including photocopying, recording, or by any information storage and retrieval system, without permission in writing from Quiet Corner Press

Cover design and interior illustrations by Steven Novak

www.novakillustration.com

ISBN: 0615793363
ISBN-13: 978-0615793368 (Quiet Corner Press)

DEDICATION

For that one time that one thing happened.
Who cares? Enough with the dedications.

ACKNOWLEDGMENTS

I've written three of these things now, three books filled with stories that make me look not too terribly cool. In a weird way it was therapeutic. It's been fun. I won't be writing any more, but it's been fun.

MY heartfelt thanks go out to everyone who helped me clean these things up and put them out there, and Mary Ann Bernal specifically for sticking with me through Volume 3.

I'll never bug any of you with this nonsense again.

I promise.

-**Steven**

LOOKS LIKE A TACO

LOOKS LIKE A TACO

Here's a little advice for the parents out there; if you're going to hire a babysitter to watch your kids, make sure the babysitter in question doesn't have anything dangling between their legs.

I'm talking about a penis, of course.

If it's a girl with one of those weird womanly messes that looks a heck of a lot like a drippy loose meat sandwich, that's fine.

I would, of course, have to question just how in the hell you happen to know what your babysitter's lady lips look like, but whatever. A little floppy meat blowing in the breeze doesn't necessarily hinder one's babysitting skills.

Why am I so against male babysitters? Well, when I was just a wee tyke, my parents hired a neighborhood teenager by the name of Al to watch my brother and I.

The name "Al" alone really should have been a dead giveaway. Despite the fact that the babysitter' name sounded more like a New York City cab driver, they still said, "Sure, Al! Sure, you can watch our children while we're out for the evening! Sure, Al! Sure, you can be the single biggest influence on their young minds! Sure, AL! Go for it, AL!"

I mean, come on - Al is the name of the local butcher. It's the name of the guy down the street with all the junk in his back yard. You know the one, the guy who doesn't seem to have a job of any kind and is often seen working on the motorcycle in his garage without a shirt on.

Babysitters are named Jennie, or Jessie, or possibly, Debbie, or other names that end in an "i.e." Not Al, though - never Al.

On one specific evening, I was heading from my bedroom and into the kitchen, while going through the living room in the process. Al was sitting on the couch. He spotted me from across the room "Hey, Steve..."

"What?"

"Come here."

I walked over to him. Suddenly, only an extremely crummy coffee table separated us. "What?"

"Look. Check this out." He said, pointing behind me and toward the television.

I remember, very distinctly, being annoyed with Al the minute he called me over. I never liked the guy. I always thought he was kind of a jerk. Now he was bothering me when I had things to do. My matchbox cars weren't going to play with themselves! The bugs outside weren't going to throw themselves in my little jam jars in order to be a part of my bug zoo! I was a busy kid. damn it!

Who did this guy think he was, bothering me with this nonsen…

When I turn around, I see it…

Sex - actual, honest to God, real life fucking.

It was in a Beta-Max format, but whatever. It was still sex.

Up to that point, my boyhood sexual fantasies had been given life, thanks mostly to the help of the bra advertisements in the Sunday paper, the Sports Illustrated Swimsuit Issue and the "saucy" artwork on my father's Tanya Tucker album. You know the one I'm talking about, right? It's the one where she's dressed in black leather pants on the cover - the one I had hiding under my bed. It's the one I pulled out every night, before I drifted off to sleep, and stared at for hours on end without blinking.

The way I stared at that thing was a lot like Hannibal Lecter - without the cannibalism.

While those had been fine and dandy, and they filled my brain with all sorts of wonderful ideas, what Al was showing me - it was something else entirely. It was actual naked people doing things that actual naked people do.

On the television screen before me were wieners and balls, and lady things and all sorts of...

Hey, look at that girl's hoo-ha. It kind of looks like a taco. I didn't think they would look like tacos.

I stood motionless in the glow of the television as the taco-crotched girl with the big lips, and even bigger boobs, gobbled away at the ding-a-ling of the square-jawed guy with the creepy mustache.

It was mesmerizing.

I wasn't "exactly" sure what I was seeing. I wasn't even sure if I liked it, or hated it, or wanted to look at it, or wanted to run away screaming. All I knew was that I couldn't look away.

Despite being disgusted, aroused, and just a smidge weirded out, I was completely and totally engrossed in what I was seeing. It was excruciating.

It was intoxicating.

From somewhere behind me, I heard Al's voice. "Hey, hey, check this out, watch this."

On the screen, the mustache man bent taco girl over a kitchen table.

THWAP! THWAP! THWAP! He slapped his tally-wacker on her butt cheeks a couple times.

Wow, look at her butt. Look at her back, and her neck and those pointy nipples on her boobs.

My crotch was getting warm.

For a moment, I even forget that there was a teenage boy in the room with me and that he was sitting behind me with a weird crooked smile on his face. He looked like a dirty, toothless, starving hobo with a turkey leg. He looked hungry.

In the presence of wet naked parts, little else but the naked parts actually mattered. (I believe that was the 11th commandment. It was on the tablet that broke.)

Then something weird happened. Instead of sticking his ding-a-la-do into her taco, mustache man slid it north and started squeezing it into her poo hole.

Really? There? What the hell? That's not where it's supposed to go, is it?

I couldn't figure out why the guy was forcing himself into the outbox when the inbox was only inches away. It didn't make sense to me – sort of like inserting Tab A into Slot C when it was made to go in Slot B. Was he confused? The girl looked Asian. Were her instructions in Japanese?

From behind me, Al mumbled, "Awwwwww yaaaaaaaaa...take that shit, bitch."

Almost on cue, on the television, mustache man said to taco girl, "Ya, fuck ya. You like that, bitch? You like that!?"

It frightened me how alike he and Al seemed to think.

Mustache man reached out, grabbed a handful of her hair and pulled. He then proceeded to smack her booty with an open hand a few times. When her ass was as red and puffy as a drunken Ted Kennedy's face, just for the hell of it, he smacked her on the back of the head. For an encore, he kicked her on the shin.

Now he was beating her up?

Turned out sex was nothing like I thought it would be – it was more like a fight. It looked a lot more painful than I'd imagined.

ZIPPPPPP.

I turned around and noticed that Al had his hand in his pants.

A second later I was gone – running down the hall as fast as my legs would take me. I scurried into my bedroom, crawled into the corner and proceeded to rock back and forth for the next half an hour while humming the Alvin and the Chipmunks Christmas song in my head.

To this very day I hate tacos.

Goats Eat Cans Volume 3

HOT WHEELS, THE DORK-ASS WAY

HOT WHEELS, THE DORK-ASS WAY

If you were born with an undeniable fascination for boobs of all shapes and sizes, a slightly odd desire to see things blow up, and, of course, a penis - then you undoubtedly played with Hot Wheels cars as a kid. You just did. It's that simple.

The sky is blue. Day turns to night. Night becomes day. You live. One day you'll die. Along the way, you'll pay taxes. If you have a penis and are under the age of four, you play with Hot Wheels. Those of you out there without a penis, for some reason, will eventually become obsessed with shoes.

These are the fundamental truths in life.

To defy even one would essentially be tampering with the very things that bind together life itself. It would be the equivalent of meeting Mother Nature herself, getting her drunk, taking her to a Motel 6 somewhere in the city, doing her up the pooper while she's unconscious, recording it and putting it online for the entire world to see.

It would be stupid.

When Mother Nature's friend stumbles onto the video and tells her about it during their Tuesday afternoon Pilate class at the local gym, she's going to be pissed. The repercussions of such a thing would be serious. You piss off Mother Nature and she'll hit you with a tsunami, or an earthquake, or a volcano, or dare I say it, a sequel to the Ben Affleck and Michael Bay plop-fest, "Pearl Harbor."

"Pearl Harbor 2: The Nagasaki Payback," or something.

When I was just a wee tyke, my younger brother and I would spend hours playing with our Hot Wheels cars.

The great thing about Hot Wheels is that even the poorest of the poor kids (which we pretty much were) could afford a Hot Wheels, now and again. Back in the day, you could buy the things almost anywhere and get them for remarkably cheap prices. The ones that looked like real cars, the futuristic ones, the special edition versions with sports hero names on them like William the Refrigerator Perry and the WWF's Big John Stud - we had them all.

Oh, and yes, I just called Big John Stud a "sports hero." I'm also aware of how stupid that sounds.

The toy aisle at the grocery store was a hot bed of cheap toys for kids, with homemade shorts for the summer months, like us.

Speaking of homemade shorts, let me take a moment to roll my eyes, shake my head and sigh deeply. The homemade shorts never really did much for my image with the ladies. What gets em' wetter than a baby seal - pretty much everything other than homemade shorts.

Anyway, in the toy aisle of the grocery store, you could find everything from water guns to stupid cups attached to balls on strings, jacks (which no one was ever really sure of what to do with), to those cheap G.I. Joe knock off figures called "C.O.R.P.S.," and, of course, Hot Wheels.

My mother could spend her sixty bucks on food for the week, snag a couple Hot wheels, bring the total up to sixty-two bucks and have her kids think of her as a hero.

Two bucks for a little hero worship - seems like a pretty good deal to me.

Unlike most kids, my brother, Nick, and I had a somewhat unique way of playing with our Hot Wheels cars. We didn't set them up on tracks, or race them around the yard. We didn't smash them together while making goofy sound effects sounds and then pretending they blew up, and that the little imaginary men inside of them ran out on fire while screaming for their mothers as their last gasps of breath escaped their lungs and their skin turned to ash.

Well, not most of the time, anyway.

You see, more often than not, my little bro and I played a game we liked to call "car lot."

What's "cat lot," you ask? Let me explain.

The game would begin with us dragging the large box that housed our Hot Wheels collection into the living room. After that, we pulled out the cars one-by-one and lined them up in rows on the carpet.

Exciting, huh?

Bet you're on the edge of your seat right about now, aren't you?

It's sort of like being in the first row at a Poison concert in 1987, right?

You know, without the possibility of getting some sort of sexually transmitted disease simply by having Vince Neil's sweat drip onto you.

Well, you better hold onto your hat, bucko. Strap yourself in and say a prayer to whatever god you believe in because the action only gets hotter from here on out!

Once all the cars were lined up all nice and straight, my brother would walk his two fingers across the carpet and toward the line.

His fingers would then stroll patiently back and forth through the rows until my two fingers stepped alongside with a smarmy look on their tiny finger-face.

My fingers would then open the conversation with something along the lines of, "So...can I help you out? Got anything specific in mind?"

"Just looking?"

"Oh, yeah? What kind of car are you looking for? How about a little something with some kick under the hood? Perhaps you'd like a smoother ride? Wait, wait, wait...I know what you want. You're looking for something to impress a lady friend, aren't you? Yep, I know you are, you old dog."

"I'm not sure. I'm just looking."

"Can I show you something really special that we just got in?"

"I'm not really. I mean, I'm just..."

"Come on. It'll only take a second. You won't regret it, trust me."

The annoyingly pushing fingers would then lead my brother's fingers over to the Big John Stud car. Ten minutes later both sets of fingers were signing papers and finalizing a deal.

That was it - that was "car lot."

This was how my brother and I "played" with our Hot Wheels.

WHEW! I told you it was exciting!

Take a minute to catch your breath and wipe the sweat from your forehead. The last thing I need is one of you dopes having a heart attack.

Okay, fine, so it wasn't really all that exciting. I can admit it. In fact, its lame – it was a lame story told by a lame man about a lame childhood.

Now I'm going to go and stick my lame head into my lame oven.

Goats Eat Cans Volume 3

THE BIG PICKLE

THE BIG PICKLE

Growing up as a "white trash" boy in the heart of the Midwest, there were a lot of exceptionally stupid things I was dragged to as a kid.

Ever been to an air show? I have.

How about a boat show? Yep, I've done that too.

When the RV show came into town, my family was the first in line.

Anything we could get into that was either incredibly cheap or flat out free, and was more often than not, the destination of the month. It didn't matter if it was even the slightest bit interesting. Don't be silly.

It's not that I don't see any redeeming qualities to an RV show.

It's just that I don't see any redeeming quality to an RV show.

(That wasn't a typo.)

In fact, I would wager that there are few things more uninteresting to a little kid than the hot new advances in camping technology.

"Hey look. This one has a sink…and a fireplace. That's pretty…cool?"

These trips were taking place around the same time that my mother would drag my brother and I to the fabric store to pick out patterns for our summer clothes.

Yep, homemade clothes. Sweet – double-sweet, even - sweet like a cool glass of sweet tea in the hands of a busty southern girl with a hand fan.

As you can imagine, I was the envy of every kid in the neighborhood. In this particular case "envy" of course means, "laughing stock."

As much as I complain, I understand that my parents were doing the best they could with what they had. What they just happened to have, was very little. I hated it then, but I can certainly understand it now.

Because it's fun to complain, I feel like I should mention the fact that there was one place, in particular, that my parents dragged me to almost every year - one place so horrible that I'm not sure I could ever forgive them for making me go. I don't care if they were broke. Being broke isn't an excuse – not for this place – not for The Renaissance Faire.

Oh, sweet lord, I hated the Renaissance Faire.

If you don't hate the Renaissance Faire, then I don't think we can be friends anymore. I want that X-Box game back that I lent you. I want those CD's too - the ones you asked to burn copies of – drop them off at my place today. I also want you to smack yourself in the head with a closed fist and call yourself an idiot. Do it. Do it right now. When you're done doing it, do it again.

Idiot.

The Renaissance Faire was worse than Brussels sprouts, or beets, or that stupid William "The Refrigerator" Perry G.I. Joe action figure. (Which was pretty bad.)

I've never understood the Renaissance Faire. *What's the point?*

Weirdo's making minimum wage, dressed up in horrible outfits that are blathering piss-poor garbled, faux English accents? No? How about those very same weirdos peddling their poorly made jewelry and remarkably shitty food? That's not working for you either?

Wait, how about the poorly thought out sideshows? For example, those two beer-bellied guys wrestling in a mud pit? Still nothing?

Maybe you'd prefer a wiener-jackass with a bow and arrow? Not even that?

If that isn't floating your boat, how about the badly choreographed joust, followed by the badly choreographed sword fight that ends with a badly choreographed kill?

No? Still not sold yet?

Yeah, I can't say I blame you.

Every time my parents tossed me in the station wagon and lugged me to this terrible excuse for entertainment, I would find myself fighting the urge to become the world's youngest suicide case.

There are only two reasons I never opened the door and flopped onto the pavement at sixty miles per hour.

The first was the fact that the faire often featured a bevy of rather chesty women with their pushed up jugs.

The second was the big pickles.

Of course, I loved the boobs. Based on everything you've read up to this point, you really should have seen that one coming. It was fairly common for me to spend my day at the faire with my jacket in front of my crotch in order to hide my baby boner.

The big pickles though, I'm thinking that one might have caught you off guard.

What the hell is a big pickle? Well, a big pickle is exactly what the name suggests – it's a really damn big pickle.

Every year at the faire, I would stumble onto a giant barrel filled to the brim with foul-smelling, sun-soaked pickle juice. Bobbing atop the awful liquid, like turds plopped by the Green Giant himself, were the big pickles.

They were as long as my head. They were as thick as a horse's johnson. As luck would have it, they were as delicious and juicy as horse dong as well.

Wait. Um.

Hold on. Er...no, wait. Forget I typed that, okay?

Please? Come on. Just forget it.

I'll tell you what, if you forget, I'll be your best friend. Deal?

I would spend the entire day walking from one end of this horribly boring faire to the other with a smile, a mile wide, on my stupid little face. All the while, my tiny fingers would be wrapped firmly around a giant green phallus symbol.

Sucking and gnawing on it's tough, yet, flexible skin.

Lathering my face in its delicious, tangy, tasty juices.

Stuffing my lips with its fullness and letting its sun-drenched insides drip down my chin.

When I was done, I'd immediately ask for another.

I made it so easy for my father to dislike me.

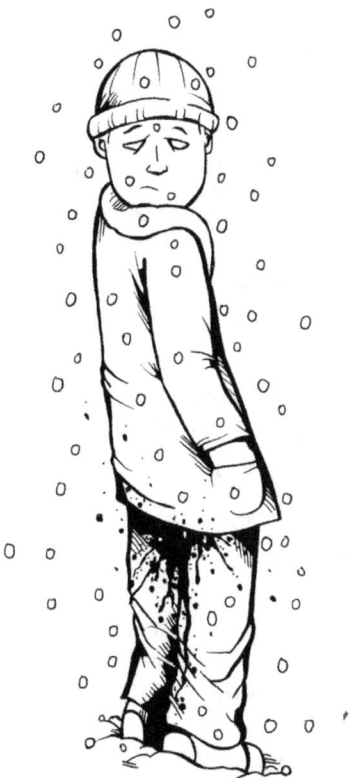

PUSSY WHERE MY WIENER SHOULD BE

PUSSY WHERE MY WIENER SHOULD BE

A group of young boys, and ten or so inches of snowfall, can be a dangerous thing. It's as simple as that.

The male of the species is generally a stupid sort of thing to begin with. You know, on account of penis' and stuff.

Boys can go from being stupid to being significantly more stupid when snow is entered into the equation, though. They get rowdy. They get mean. Their already impaired judgment becomes idiotically impaired. They begin posturing, and posturing generally leads to an undeniable desire to show off.

Snow does this for boys and strip clubs do it for men.

I think a discount at Denny's does it for the elderly.

Don't quote me on that, though.

It was only a fifteen-minute walk from the house I grew up in and a short jog past the baseball fields to the town's old rock quarry. The place hadn't been used in years.

If you happened to be a homeless man - possibly with the word "boxcar" attached to his name - it was a pretty decent spot to start a bonfire and eat canned beans. It was also a make-out spot for horny teenagers not quite old enough to own a car, a place for kids to set off illegal fireworks and a perfect little hideaway for anyone looking to get rid of something they didn't want anymore.

People would dump everything in this place: Stereos, food, a car, farm equipment, the bodies of their victims - everything.

The walls of the quarry were littered with rusted and sharp, and generally altogether scary, pieces of steel, wood and plastic.

There's a good chance there were a couple of syringes down there as well.

Did I forget to mention the local "tweakers" liked to sit at the bottom and do whatever it is tweakers do best?

I didn't?

Well, I should have - because they did.

So anyway, the tweaker-makeout-body dumping quarry sounds like the perfect place for a boy and his friends to go sledding, right?

Especially after a heavy snow when all the cars and tractors and pointy edged things are hidden underneath the Christmastime goodness, right?

Right? No?

What's that? You're thinking to yourself, "Of course not, stupid. That would be just plain stupid, stupid."

Well, you're right.

Also, stop calling me stupid.

"You go first." That was my friend, Derek.

He handed me a saucer sled and pointed toward the bottom of the quarry. Even as a young boy, I could see the folly of the idea. To sit my ass on a thin piece of plastic and throw myself down the side of a junk-laden quarry was a moronic idea, at best.

More moronic than that album Don Johnson recorded in the 80's.

I mean, I could easily have fallen off and found myself impaled on the business end of a 1978 Volkswagen Rabbit. How stupid would that look in my obituary the next morning?

I handed the sled back to Derek and shook my head. "Fuck you. You go first."

He immediately shoved it back into my chest and smacked it, once more, to make his point. "What are you, a girl? Don't be a pussy, you pussy! I'm not going first, you go first, pussy!"

My other friends were watching us and keeping their mouths shut. I'm guessing they were silently hoping that the sled didn't get shoved in their direction. Derek took note of their non-action and decided to use it to his advantage. He was going to rally the troops.

Young boys being natural followers, he knew they would instantly fall into line.

"Steve's like a little girl or something! Check him out, guys! He's all scared and stuff! He's got a pussy where his wiener should be!"

What? What did he just say? Pussy where my wiener should be?

PUSSY WHERE MY WIENER SHOULD BE!?

I didn't quite understand the logistics of it, but I sure as heck knew I wasn't going to let anyone say that about me! Not now and not ever! I had a wiener! I'd seen it before – many times, in fact!

I'd show him who had a wiener!

I snagged the sled from between us, walked to the edge of the quarry and dropped it in the snow. Everyone and everything went quiet. The wind flapped my hair and I sniffed a leaky booger back into my nose.

Plopping myself onto the sled, I grabbed hold of the sides and stared into the deceivingly smooth whiteness below. It was like dog plop covered in white chocolate – tasty, and smooth and delicious – until you open your mouth and take a big ol' bite.

By then, you're chomping down on nutty canine poop and it's too late to go back.

You can never go back from that.

With the voice of a boy firmly aware of the whereabouts of his wiener, I looked over my shoulder and growled confidently, "Someone give me a push."

Within seconds, Derek's hands were on my shoulders and he was pushing me toward the edge.

Before I knew it, I was sailing down the wall of the quarry and, most likely, breaking a few Olympic bobsled records in the process. The wind smacked me in the face and stung my boogery nose. The sled bobbed up and down, slid from side to side and threatened to toss me from its smooth, plastic surface.

I hit a mound of snow and briefly became airborne.

I was doing it! I was really doing it! I was making that quarry hill my bitch!

I was riding it like a gimp with a ball gag at a gay brothel!

Oh yea, my wiener was firmly in its place! It was right where it was supposed to be! I WAS THE MOTHER FUCKING MA...

AGH!

I spun. I flipped and I did a triple turn with a kick out and a 360 rotation that would have made Tony Hawk blush. I completed the routine by slamming my head into something buried beneath the snow, Greg Louganis style.

Just as quick as my wiener-proving adventure started, it was over.

The snow and the awful things hidden underneath became a pillow for my face. I was cold. I was sore from head to toe, and I was just a teensy bit embarrassed.

I could vaguely hear my friends yelling something at me from the top of the hill, but I couldn't quite make it out.

It sounded like, "Holy shit, you're reading like crazy?"

Sure, my read-abilities were legendary around town, but what the hell were they talking about? Reading? I wasn't reading?

I propped myself up on my hands, wiped the snow from my face, turned around and looked in their direction. Behind me, a sharp piece of metal was sticking out of the snow. From the tip of it and toward where I was sitting, were deep red blotches splattered across the snow.

I reached underneath myself and felt around a bit until I found a thick gash in my snow pants. I stuck my finger inside and wiggled it around.

Not only did my finger go inside my snow pants and the pants underneath, it went right inside the warm flesh of my butt as well – and I'm not talking about the crack.

God damn it.

My ass was torn open.

My "friends" at the top of the hill stared at me for a moment, then turned and ran away.

Bunch of jerks.

Those guys totally had pussies where their wieners should be.

-Steven Novak-

TOO MUCH INFORMATION?

TOO MUCH INFORMATION?

I'm not even sure how I found it, but I did.

Like some useless, drunken forty-niner stumbling backasswards into gold, or when Larry Appleton was forced to room with his cousin from Mypos, Balki Bartokomous, I made a discovery that would forever change the course of my life from that point on.

Also, yes - I realize I just made a "Perfect Strangers" reference. What of it? You wanna' start something? If you wanna' start something, we can start something, slappy. My left hand was made for starting and my right for finishing – in more ways than one.

Want proof? Just keep reading.

It was in the perfect hiding place - a homemade VHS copy of the movie "Another 48 Hours." It was a movie that no one, anywhere, would ever want to watch. It was the sort of movie that they showed to the prisoners at Abu Ghraib. It was terrible and it was torture.

Strip you down and trot you around naked?

How about a pair of pliers to your fingernails?

Maybe attach the business end of a car battery to your nut sack?

Too easy.

No, let's just make them watch Eddie Murphy and Nick Nolte tear up the screen as Reggie and Jack in what may be the single worst buddy movie in the history of buddy movies.

They'll tell us whatever the hell we ask them to after that. That'll rip the secrets right out of you and leave behind a hole so gaping it'll be signed, *John Holmes was here* underneath.

Yep, that was another old-timey reference. Keep yer' yap shut.

If you could actually make it through the movie, and then had the gumption to sit through the credits and a good five minutes of static, you'd find it.

Porno.

It was my parents hidden porno and I'd stumbled onto it.

Sure, the fact that it belonged to my parents was admittedly disturbing, but porno is porno and porno is even more porno when you're a little kid.

Now that I think of it, porno is porno when you're nearly thirty as well, and I imagine it still is when you're in your sixties. The classics never die.

As much as I wanted to watch it the moment I discovered it, everyone was home and it would have been impossible. Instead I rewound the tape a bit, put it back in its case and piled it by all the other movies on the shelf in the living room.

Then, I waited.

Like a cop on a stakeout for a collar so big it might make his career and set him for life within the department, I was patient.

Days passed, and then weeks. Never had a hyperactive boy been so calm and focused on a task in front of him in. I had to keep my eyes on the prize, though. I had to stay focused and stay sharp, and keep frosty.

My time would come.

The porno gods were testing me. They wanted to find out how much I really wanted it. They had to be sure I was worthy.

My hands coiled into fists and I raised them to the sky. "BRING IT ON PORNO GODS! GIMMIE EVERYTHING YOU GOT! I CAN TAKE IT! I CAN TAKE IT ALL! I'LL WAIT AN ETERNITY FOR THIS!"

They heard me, and they cowered.

I would not relent.

Then, the day arrived. I was alone in the house and alone with my mystery-parents porn. Finally.

I went into the living room and pulled the tape out of its case. Next, I had to fast-forward through the ending credits for "Another 48 Hours." It was all that stood between the sweet, delicious porno, burnt onto that reel of tape and hidden behind a few minutes of static, and me.

The first scene in the movie featured two "*struggling students*" cleaning some older woman's garage to make a little money to pay for school - pretty much your standard porno set-up.

It wasn't long before the twenty-eight-year-old *students* went from cleaning the old broad's garage to getting their schlongs cleaned by her mouth and taking turns cleaning her crotch with those very same tools.

This, of course, made everyone dirty, once again. It's the circle of life.

I was transfixed.

My mouth was hanging open, a thick strand of drool dribbling over my lower lip and onto my chin. I stared into the screen with a pair of freakish, serial killer-like, unblinking eyes. You could have tossed a straight jacket on me, locked me in a padded cell and made me say the *"fava beans and Chianti"* line. I would have fit right in.

The next scene featured another *"struggling student"* and another older woman. The kid goes from cleaning her pool to screwing her on the pool table in her husband's game room.

From the pool, to the pool table. Nice wordplay, Mr. Porno.

Unexpectedly, something began to stir in the general area of my crotch. Suddenly, there's a cucumber in my pants - or, at least, a baby gherkin.

Everything down there was tighter. My shorts didn't quite fit anymore. For reasons I couldn't quite explain, I was starting to feel embarrassed. I knew there was no one else in the house with me, and yet I felt compelled to double check.

Which is exactly what I did.

I walked from room to room with my hand over the erection in my pants. I opened every door and even looked inside the closets. I didn't find anyone. When I return to the living room, the porno had moved onto another scene.

Some woman that looked old enough to be my grandmother seemed to have some kind of hair caught in the filter of her hot tub. Another *"struggling student"* came to her rescue. Another screw session commenced.

It wasn't exactly *high art*, but who cares. There were dongs and there were lady parts, and they were sometimes being rubbed together. There were a whole host of other juices being created too, some of which were being drank and others just splattered on people's faces It was based on a plot that has worked fairly well since the dawn of man.

If it ain't broke, don't fix it, right?

As I watched, the aching feeling in my groin was getting stronger. I reached down and started to rub myself over my pants.

RUB, RUB, RUB.

Long sort of rub with a bit of a twist.

RUB, RUB, RUB.

That's pretty much all it took.

My head filled with happy gas. White, fluffy clouds floated into the space in-between the back of my eyes and tickled my brain with the funny little feathers sticking from the opposite end. I sucked in as much air as I could hold, and I rolled onto my back. My toes curled and my legs locked. My mouth opened wide and my whole body began to shake.

A sound so pathetic and high, it could easily have been confused for something made by a titmouse (he, he…I typed tit) escaped my lips.

A moment later my pants were filled with millions and millions of my superheated, little squiggly babies.

More than likely, they were excited to finally be doing what they were made to do – anxious to stretch their tales and find themselves an egg to plow their way into.

You know, until they ran into the denim interior of my jeans and immediately died.

I could almost hear them cursing my name with their final spermy breaths.

Once my head cleared, I rewound the tape, once again, put it back in its case, stacked it on the shelf, and immediately went into the bathroom to clean up.

I did the very same thing the next day - and a couple days after that - and a few after that.

Heroin isn't this addictive.

Now you know the story of my very first orgasm.

Not that you particularly wanted to, but well, you do – so, too bad.

What's done is done.

Once you learn it, it can't be unlearned – like the term, *spermy breath.*

I bet you'll never forget, *spermy breath.*

Goats Eat Cans Volume 3

DEREK AND HIS EXPLODING PROJECTILE NOGGIN

DEREK AND HIS EXPLODING PROJECTILE NOGGIN

I was eleven and her name was Elizabeth. I was pretty obsessed with her at the time.

Or, wait. You know what? Why don't we scratch that and revise.

I was eleven and her name was Elizabeth. I was pretty obsessed with her boobs at the time.

Honestly, the rest of her didn't really matter all that much to me. Her face might as well have been a sack of laundry, and the idiotic words spewing from her mouth a bunch of old socks.

I was eleven, I was stupid, and I was obsessed with boobs. I'm not ashamed of it. Hugh Hefner got to walk around his whole life in a bathrobe because of the same problem.

Liz was one of those girls that grew up chest-wise at a very early age. The flesh attached to her ribcage was age twenty-one, while the rest of her wouldn't catch up for at least ten years.

As you can imagine, this automatically made her the object of desire of every single boy in the sixth grade - whether she liked it, or not.

She didn't even need to talk. In fact, it was better if she didn't because she was actually kind of dopey. She also had that annoying, gross, mullet-sporting, confederate flag hanging in the garage, sort of white trashy thing going on.

You know what I mean, right?

Let's just say that in twenty years or so, you could easily imagine a family of raccoon's taking up residence in the underbrush of her cooch.

Get it now?

No?

That just confused you more?

Plus, you thought it was inappropriate and gross?

Ah, well, screw it.

Moving on.

"You know what, dude? We should call you Elizabeth."

That was my friend, Derek. Even at eleven, the kid had very little else on his mind other than the fairer sex. This little bastard was a prodigy. He was the Mozart of awkward boyish affections and ill-timed boners.

"What? Why?"

That was me. Even at eleven, not only did I not have any idea how to get a female's attention, but I was also simultaneously scared shitless of them. I wasn't a prodigy. I was an idiot. I was the Michael Bay of everything, Michael Bay does.

"Yeah, man. Call her. Do you have her number?"

That was Brian, a mutual friend of ours from school. As you can tell by his response, he was just a bit smoother than I was. In fairness though, I guess that isn't really saying much.

The three of us were *hanging out* at Derek's house, just relaxing in his bedroom a few days before Halloween. Derek crawled across his bed, reached over me and snagged the phone on his dresser.

"Fuck it. I'm calling her." He started dialing. He was reading the number off of a piece of folded up paper on the desk, and I was sweating while watching him.

Brian hopped off the chair at the opposite end of the room and bolted for the door. "I'm going upstairs to listen on the other phone!"

I took off after him. As we ascended the staircase, we were giggling so girlishly you'd have thought we were the ones squeezing into our first training bras.

The other phone was in the kitchen upstairs, by the time we picked up the receiver it was already ringing on the other end. We clonked our heads together like a Three Stooges routine, struggling to listen, while at the same time covering our mouths in a desperate attempt to contain the chuckles.

It was a pathetic, girlish sight.

Really pathetic, actually.

It was like something you might expect to see painted on the cover of a Sweet Valley High novel.

"Hello?"

"Is Elizabeth there?"

"Can I ask who's calling?"

"Derek."

"One second, Derek."

There was a pause.

A snort of laughter shot through Brian's gut and exploded from his mouth like a taco burp. He handed me the phone and stumbled to the opposite end of the kitchen to catch his breath and stifle his girlish glee.

"Hello?"

"Elizabeth?"

"Yes."

"Hey, it's Derek."

"I know."

"Hey."

Another pause. For all his talk, Derek wasn't nearly as smooth with the ladies as he'd let on.

"So, um...what do you want?"

"Um..."

Brian finally wrangled his chuckles and hobbled back to the phone to listen beside me. We clonked heads again and bit our tongues in order to keep from crying out in pain.

"Well, what did you call for, Derek?"

"Um..."

Derek was blowing it. He was widely considered to be the Gene Simmons of the playground, but he was blowing it worse than a blind hooker with no hands and a tiny mouth being forced to give fellatio Burt Bacharach while doing a handstand.

"Derek, are you still there? Hello?"

"You know that Steve likes you, right?"

Fucking shit.

That little asshole.

That dirty little Hockey playing, piece of shit asshole in Rollerblades.

What the hell did he think he was doing?

"Steve? Are you serious?"

"Yeah, he told me the other day that he really likes you. Said he wanted to date you and stuff."

I wanted to date, her? And stuff? What stuff?

"Really?"

"Yep."

    I tossed the phone in Brian's direction and took off for the stairs After descending them in record time, I plowed my way back into in Derek's room. As soon as I was inside, I started making choking and punching motions in his direction. I pointed at him and nodded. My jaw locked and my brows narrowed. An awful mix of anger, coupled with embarrassment, had turned me a shade red that I didn't think possible.

    I was going to kill him. I was going to wrap my fingers around his throat and squeeze until his head popped off, shooting across the room like the cork of a wine bottle and smacking his dog, Kelsey, right in the head. It would probably give her a concussion; probably kill her on the spot.

    That's how mad I was – dead dog mad.

"Totally. He told me during lunch last week. He said that he thinks you're hot...also sweet and stuff."

I couldn't hear what she was saying to him anymore. In that instant, as much as I hated Derek for doing what he was doing, a part of me needed, very badly, to hear how Liz would respond.

There was only one choice.

Back upstairs, back into the kitchen and back to smacking heads with Brian, one more time.

"So, what do you think about him?"

"I don't know."

"What do you mean? Do you like him, too?"

"I don't know. It's just, well. I don't know. He's kinda ugly."

That bitch.

That freakishly big-boobed, eleven-year-old, jerk.

Brian made one of those *"ouch"* faces, handed the phone over to me and stepped away. When his back turned, his shoulders began to shake. I could have sworn he was laughing.

Feeling like I'd just been punched in the gut, I immediately hung up the phone.

I pictured myself squeezing Derek's neck again, and his head popping off again. While I imagined it still hit Kelsey, this time it ricocheted off the dog, smashed through the living room window, sailed two miles through the air and crashed through Elizabeth's window where it exploded for reasons that really made no sense.

Maybe it hit a gas line or something, I don't know.

It could happen.

Shut up, it was my fantasy.

If I wanted it to explode, set her dog on fire and kill everyone in her family that's exactly what it would do.

Screw you.

Also, screw that broad.

A few days later, on Halloween night, while out with Derek and Brian, I decided to venture off on my own. I strolled across town to Elizabeth's house, snatched the pumpkins off of her front porch, and smashed them on her driveway.

Then I convinced myself that her boobs were lopsided, anyway.

Stupid weird-breasted, weirdo.

Lopsidey.

Yeah, that's what I was going to call her – lopsidey.

I felt better – I guess – sort of.

In an ugly sort of way.

RED AS A DEVIL

RED AS A DEVIL

Kids believe in a lot of really stupid stuff.

They have Santa Claus and The Easter Bunny. There's a baby delivering stork and the Care Bears, Luke Skywalker, world peace, that Justin Bieber has talent, and even that their parents actually love each other.

I guess the point that I'm trying to make is that kids, in general, are dummies.

Okay, so adults are fairly stupid as well, but it's a whole different kind of stupid.

Or, wait. Is it any different?

Screw it, sideways.

Everyone is an idiot.

I guess it's only fair that I admit the above gibberish was an extremely sad attempt to come up with a poignant little opening for my story that not only relates to the upcoming text, but makes a statement and provides a little comedy to boot.

Obviously, I've failed miserably.

Not only did I fail, but I'm now making an extra effort to point out the fact that I failed, which, in turn, has transformed a regular, run of the mill failure into something I feel justified with adding the word *epic* to.

Remember when Rosie O'Donnell played a *mentally handicapped* woman in that made for television movie? That's how bad this opening was. It was that bad, times two. It was sort of like a naked cripple chick with leg braces that crawls out of the cake at your bachelor party.

Sure, she's got nice boobs. She also can't walk, and it's more than a little bit sad watching her end up face down in the cooler, covered in cheap beer and crying because she busted her tooth.

That'll counter-act a boob-boner every time.

Okay, I think that's just about enough of this nonsense - time for the main-event.

"Hey, you know what we should do? Play red as a devil."

That was my friend, Derek. He, myself and a few of our friends were sitting in the front yard of my house trying to come up with something to waste the day away, other than the usual lounging around, riding bikes and possibly watching some television.

The good ol' days.

Our pal, Mike was the first to respond. "What's red as a devil?"

"It's cool, man. My older brother and his friends do it all the time, and stuff. Everyone, get your asses over here. Kind of get in a circle."

We crowded around Derek. "Okay, now one of us has to stand in the middle of the circle."

Everyone looked to the person on either side rather than moving. No one wanted to get in the middle, and I honestly couldn't blame them. Derek had a bit of a reputation and there was a fairly decent chance that getting in the middle meant becoming the butt of one of his stupid pranks. Before you knew it, you'd find yourself being held down on the grass with Derek standing above you. He'd drop his pants, squat on your face and blast a wet-one right up your nostrils.

We called it the brown wash.

In my head I reminded myself that I was much bigger than Derek, and most of my friends, for that matter. I could easily toss him off me if he attempted to launch a chocolate-dandy in my direction.

"I'll do it."

"Awesome. Once Steve's in the middle, everyone needs to hold hands and close the circle around him."

The group held hands and the circle closed.

"Okay, now close your eyes. Clear your mind, and stuff. I mean, like totally empty it, guys. Once it's empty, we're going to start moving in a circle around him and when you do that, you have to think about the devil. Picture him in your mind…the horns and the tail and all that shit. When you've got a clear picture, you need to repeat the words *red as a devil,* over and over again until the devil takes over his body."

Not a single one of us bothered to question the absurdity of it all.

Not one of us.

Which is sad.

Don't get me wrong, I was well aware of the fact that my friends were massive idiots, but this was taking it a bit far – even for those dolts.

This was the sort of nonsense girls do at slumber parties.

The next thing you know, we'd be braiding each other's hair, painting our nails and talking about boys in our *My Little Pony* pajamas. Maybe we'd even finish off the evening with a rousing game of truth or dare? How about trying to get each other to levitate off of the dining room table?

Maybe our periods would even align with the cycle of the moon.

There I was, standing in the middle of the circle and listening to my pals chant, *red as a devil,* over and over and over again, while at the same time, trying to keep from laughing. It was at this moment, I was struck with an idea.

"Red as a devil, red as a devil, red as a devil."

I closed my eyes tight and started making weird moaning noises.

"Red as a devil, red as a devil, red as a devil."

I stopped moaning and let loose a half growl, half scream - not so much that it came off as obviously fake, but still enough to make them take notice.

"Red as a devil, red as a devil."

My body started shaking – because I started shaking it. I dropped to my knees, put my fists on my head and tried my best to seem like I was dealing with some otherworldly pain. I popped my eyes open and grit my teeth. I wanted to make them think my head was about to explode like that dude from the beginning of *Scanners*.

"Red as a-"

"Agh!" It was a louder scream than I'd ever screamed in my life.

I leapt from my knees, shoved Derek in the chest and sent him sailing into the bushes.

Between you and me, that was really the highlight of the day.

My remaining friends unlocked hands and took off running. Mike bolted toward the front door of my house, Jimmy scurried behind a tree and David was already half way down the block. Mike was the slowest, so naturally I ran after him.

Hot on his tail, I made sure to allow a fair amount of drool and foamy spit seep from the side of my mouth and catch the breeze. I looked like a dog with rabies, or a girl giving an exceptionally messy blowjob, or a girl giving an exceptionally messy blowjob to a dog with rabies.

Mike opened the screen door, slammed it behind him and locked the little locking mechanism on the handle. Mere seconds behind him, yelling and generally making an ass of myself, I snagged the door handle, and gave it a tug.

It broke right off.

SNAP.

As if it were made of that stale old gum they used to stuff into packs of baseball cards.

What the hell?

Was it because of hell – literally?

The damn thing snapped right off - like a dried out old twig, or the corpse of Macho Man Randy Savage snapping into a Slim Jim.

I didn't remember being strong enough to snap metal in two.

My hooting and hollering stopped and I looked down at the broken handle in my hand. I was like The Incredible Hulk, or at the very least a roided up, Lou Ferrigno sporting a pair of shredded purple pants.

Even my friends - who kind of knew I was just screwing around – were suddenly looking at me with my broken screen door handle and wondering what to make of the situation.

Was I actually possessed by the devil? Did he take control of my soul for a brief moment and fill me with the strength of the deepest, darkest pit of hell? Was I the anti-Christ, and it took some unassuming children's game to make me aware of my evil origins? Would I, one day, usher in a million years of pain for all who call Earth home?

How awesome would that be?

If I was the anti-Christ, then my old man gave the anti-Christ a hell of a spanking about an hour and a half later. My ass was red for hours.

Red as a devil, even.

-Steven Novak-

MY FIRST KISS AND MY FIRST BREAK-UP

MY FIRST KISS AND MY FIRST BREAK-UP

Her parents owned a restaurant just outside of town called *Wine and Spirits*. She had long, light-brown hair that curled near the bottom, brown eyes and dimples so cute they would have made a panda barf. Her name was Debbie and she was not only my very first *real* crush, but my first kiss and my first break-up as well.

That's right, she's got the Steve trifecta, ladies!

Honestly, I'm not the least bit sure what that was supposed to mean. I really should think about things before I type them.

Debbie and her family lived on the opposite side of town – the *rich folk* side – the part of town where they extended their pinky fingers when they drank their *Bartles and James.*

Bartles and James? Really? Did I just make a *Bartles and James* reference? Who the hell is even going to remember that stuff?

Ignoring my moronic callback to some forgotten 80's nostalgia, my relationship with Debbie was the one and only time in my life where I was the "*bad boy from the wrong side of the tracks*" for a girl.

Sure, I was only in sixth grade, but come on, just let me have this one.

Considering the way the rest of my life went, let me have just this one. Please? Just once?

I'll be your best friend.

On one particularly sticky summer day when Debbie's parents were away, I was sitting on the couch at her house with another girl named Jennifer. and my good pal, Derek. We weren't really doing much – mostly just talking and acting awkward around the opposite sex in that very specific sixth-grader sort of way.

The boredom led to a Ouija Board – as boredom so often does.

From the instant it was out, and we had our hands on it, Derek and I began using it to spell out things like "*shit*" and "*boobs.*" I think we even tossed out a *"shittyboob."*

Truly groundbreaking comedy.

Out of the blue, Derek chimed in with, "Hey Debbie, Steve was telling me the other day that he really wanted to kiss you."

What the hell? Are you kidding me? Where did that come from?

Don't get me wrong; it was totally true, but that little putz, Derek, shouldn't have just spit it out like that. Where the hell did he get off? Who did he think he was?

I'd actually told Derek that I wanted to do a lot more than simply kiss Debbie, so I guess I should have considered myself lucky that, at the very least, he decided not to go into the grizzly details.

"Hey, Debbie, Steve was telling me the other day that he really wanted to stick his wiener in your mouth, have you tug on his balls, and pump away at his johnson until he finishes on your face."

If he'd said that to her, it might not have gone over as well.

Just call it a hunch.

Debbie seemed a bit surprised by my pal's sudden explosion of private information. She was squirming in her seat. She looked uncomfortable. "What?"

"He said that he really wanted to kiss you. He thinks you've been going together for a while now and he wa…"

"Shut up, Man!" I punched him in the shoulder with all my strength and sent him over the arm of the couch and onto the floor.

Good. He deserved that punch. I was glad it hurt. I had to shut him up. I had to. Derek was a good friend, but he really needed to shut the hell up. Enough was enough. The kid was burying me. A very large part of me wanted to lean over and punch him again - this time in the leg – maybe in the head to really fuc…

"Okay." That was Debbie. She interrupted my daydream of beating the hell out of my friend to say *okay.*

Wait, she said okay?

She said okay? She said okay to the idea of kissing me? She agreed to it? She agreed to kiss me? Me?

I looked over at her and she was smiling at me. Her head tilted to the side just a bit, in an extremely cute, super-embarrassed sort of way. Derek immediately stopped screaming about his injured arm and sat up. He was as surprised as me at the way the situation had unfolded.

I'm thinking he was just a little bit jealous too.

This made up for the fact that I didn't get to punch him in the leg.

I tried to say something to Debbie, but there was a lump in my throat the size of grown man's fully erect penis. (Not that I would know or anything.)

I swallowed it down (the same as you would, if there was a grown man's fully erect penis in your mouth) steadied my nerves and managed to form something vaguely resembling an actual word. "Really?"

"Yeah, Sure."

She stood up and took my hand. "But not here. Let's go out back."

A second later she was leading me toward the back door as Derek and Jennifer watched in stunned silence.

Once outside, we sat across from each other in a couple of chairs on her deck. After a minute or so of staring and giggling like a couple of embarrassed *Care Bears* in a Saturday morning cartoon, I took a deep breath and leaned in close.

My hands were sweaty.

I couldn't seem to figure out where to put them.

Was I supposed to touch her face? It seemed like people were always touching faces when they made out in the movies. No, I couldn't touch her face – not with my sweaty ass hands. She'd be grossed out.

For the briefest of moments, I considered reaching out and touching her boob nubbins, then quickly decided that probably wasn't the way to go – at least if I ever wanted to kiss her again.

Before I knew what I was doing, my hands ended up on her shoulders. Grabbing them like I was like giving her a massage from the front, squeezing and kneading her flesh so hard it probably hurt, and likely left her bruised. It was awkward as all hell.

I immediately forgot about my angry massage-man hands when her lips touched mine.

They felt soft – warm and soft, and absolutely nothing like the *Teela* cartoon on the He-Man pillow I practiced smooching on every night before sleep.

It was weird – mashing my lips against the lips of another human being. I was enjoying it, but I wasn't entirely sure why.

Ten seconds passed.

Ten turned to twenty and twenty rolled into thirty.

Now what the hell am I supposed to do?

Neither of us moved. We just sat there, breathing through our mouths as the trees swayed overhead. My eyes were wide open and I was staring into her closed eyelids with my hands still tugging at the flesh of her shoulders like I was pulling weeds.

A chipmunk ran past. He stopped on the fence to the right and stared at us while nibbling away at something he'd snagged from a nearby tree.

For a second I almost thought I could see the little bastard laughing.

How long was this supposed to last?

I'd seen people kiss in the movies and they sometimes did it for a long time, but they were squirming and rubbing, and letting their tongues do all sorts of crazy stuff. Debbie and I were just sitting there.

It was beginning to get awkward.

I was moments away from extending my tongue forward, wiggling it around and hoping for the best when Debbie pulled away from me and opened her eyes. She had a weird half smile on her face. She looked like she sort of, kind of enjoyed our confusing embrace and was sort of, kind of freaked out by the whole thing.

It's the same look people make after eating a whole box of Kraft Macaroni and Cheese on their own. While the first twenty spoonfuls are tasty enough, the second twenty make you want to kill yourself.

BANG! BANG! BANG!

What the hell was that?

I turned to my left and spotted Derek pressed against the back window with his hands in the air. "WHOOO! YA! AWESOME!"

Unless they'd gone and changed the definition of the word *awesome*, I could not have possibly disagreed with him more.

He dropped his pants, turned around, squashed his ass against the window and let loose a blast of air that rattled the glass.

Fantastic.

It was the absolute perfect period on the end of the sentence that was my first kiss.

About a month later, Debbie told me that she and her family were moving out of state. Falsely believing myself to be that hottest shit since *The Human Torch* took a flaming shit – you know, mostly because I was the first person in my group of friends to kiss a girl – I informed Debbie that that I *couldn't deal with a long-term relationship* (whatever the hell that's supposed to mean when you're in sixth grade) and broke up with her. (Whatever the hell that's supposed when you're in sixth grade.)

By the time I was in the eighth grade, she'd moved back into town.

In the two years she'd been gone, my home life had gone to shit. I was depressed. I had no friends, and I spent most of my day drawing pictures of me killing myself.

Believe it or not, Debbie had no interest in pressing our lips together awkwardly for old time's sake.

It's probably better that she didn't.

Though my *Teela* pillow was pretty faded and worn, I'm fairly confident my technique hadn't improved.

-Steven Novak-

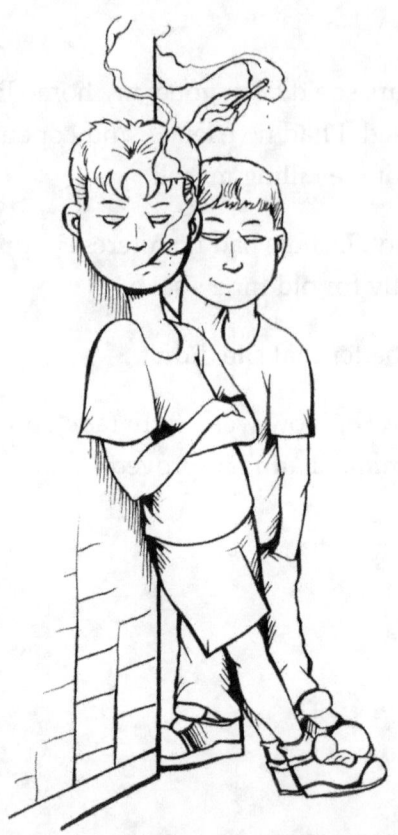

BACK WHEN I WAS COOLER THAN FONZIE

BACK WHEN I WAS COOLER THAN FONZIE

"Do you think we could smoke it? Dude, I totally dare you to smoke one of those."

That was my friend, Derek. We were about ten-years-old and we were hanging out near the bleachers at the baseball field in the center of town. The thing he was daring me to smoke was one of the cigarette butts lying in the sand by his feet.

Yeah, that's right, a used and discarded cigarette butt.

Of course, common sense told me there was no way in hell anyone, anywhere should ever snatch a used cigarette butt off the ground, stick it in their mouth, light it up and smoke it. It was a stupid idea. It was idiotic. The thing was likely home to more disease than the combined crotches of Paris Hilton, Kim Kardashian and Jenna Jameson combined.

It was a festering pool of diseased nastiness.

It was a disaster waiting to happen.

It was a lose-lose situation.

It was a romantic comedy, Katherine Heigl.

Even knowing it was disgusting, and wrong and just flat out gross, what do you think I did?

Well, I did what any exceptionally stupid young kid trying his damndest to be *cool* would do in the same situation. I pulled it from the sand, fired it up and puffed away at all of the disgusting badness inside.

The smoke tasted sort of like an omelet - like an egg-white omelet cooked to perfection up on the space in between Star Jones' boobs.

As a boy, I was a complete and total pushover when it came to the concept of *cool*. I would've gone anywhere, done anything and killed anyone for *coolness*. I would have punched *The Incredible Hulk* in his face or urinated on *Superman's* cape.

Want proof? Let's fast forward to a month or so later.

A mutual friend by the name of Sarah, suggested we break into her grandparent's house (who also happened to be the Mayor) and have a little *party*.

Breaking and entering? Really? This was a major step up for me.

I should have laughed in Sarah's face. I should have punched Derek in the junk (which rhymes) and screamed, "*NO*" like I was being offered a joint in some 80's afterschool special. Instead, I sputtered and squeaked the following sentence as if my balls were still waiting to drop.

"Su-sur-sure, Sarah. Le-let's do it."

Here's the deal; Sarah was older than the both of us by quite a few years. She had actual, fully formed boobs instead of the nipple puffs girls our own age were sporting. Most importantly she was "*cool.*"

She was *cool* and she was attractive and the thought of committing a felony with someone *cool* automatically made me think I was cool by proxy.

Isn't that how it works? No?

Oh well, even if it didn't, I was pretty hypnotized by her tits.

Yep, that's right - I'm blaming it on the chest balloons.

Men have been doing it for centuries.

When all else fails, blame it on the tits.

A couple days later, it was B&E time.

Okay...so maybe it wasn't exactly a B&E – Sarah, did have a key. It just sounds so much *cooler* to call it a full-fledged B&E.

So, um, forget I brought up the key. Let's pretend that I smashed in the window with a rock or something.

Yeah, a big giant rock - there was glass everywhere. I had to punch a Doberman in the face after I climbed in the window and I knocked him out with a single blow.

Hell, yeah! I'm such a hard ass.

Once we were inside, myself, Derek, Sarah and a friend she brought along, broke the lock on the liquor cabinet in the basement.

Okay, scratch that. We didn't so much *break the lock* as smash the door with a crowbar we found his garage. (I'm actually not lying about that part. That's pretty badass, right?)

It was like, Wonka's Chocolate factory in there - you know, without the Oompa Loomaps, and if the Fizzy Lifting Drink was actually Jack Daniels.

If Agustus Gloop had fallen into the river at that factory, fugedaboutit. No twelve step program on earth would have saved his dimpled ass.

At ten-years-old, I didn't know rum from whiskey or whiskey from a bottle filled with piss and left in the sun for a week, but I was pretty sure that anything with 100 Proof on it was the *cool* stuff.

Sarah was watching. I needed the *cool* stuff.

We spent the day cracking open everything in the cabinet, tasting, drinking, laughing and pouring whatever remained on the carpet in the basement. We sprayed the walls of the hallway and even created a little liquor river that rolled down the stairs.

Derek took a dump in one of the potted plants in the bedroom, but that's a whole other story.

When we finished vandalizing the mayor's house, we decided to call it a day and head for home. At least, I think that's what we decided to do.

I was pretty hammered.

That night, it felt like there were two rhinos engaging in some nasty, hardcore, freaky-scary loving in my stomach. There was also a Beluga whale wedged between the folds of my brain watching it all and beating himself off.

His Beluga dong was slippery. His fin kept sliding off and whacking against the interior of my skull. Plus, he was having a hard time finishing.

As you can imagine, a pair of rhino's don't exactly make for a top-notch porno.

At about one in the morning, I ended up on the toilet with tsunami-esque diarrhea blasting from between my buttocks with more force than hurricane Katrina.

The pressure in my ass sprinted toward my mouth. To avoid puking on my parents floor, I slid off the toilet, spun around and unleashed a firehose-like spray of vomit into the already poop-filled toilet.

And yes, if you really need to know - there was some serious splash back.

I felt like shit.

I smelled like shit.

I had nutty, booze-marinated shit particles in my hair.

Being cool kicks ass.

-Steven Novak-

FRACTURED RIBS AND PISS POOR FIBS

FRACTURED RIBS AND PISS POOR FIBS

After my parents divorced, things got a little weird between my old man and I.

Honestly, I'm not entirely sure that my father was ever really interested in being a Dad. Don't get me wrong, he probably learned to accept it and might have even found some things he liked about it, eventually. I'm just not sure that having to take care of a useless bundle of crying and poop was necessarily in his thirty-year plan.

The dude was pretty young at the time. I think he might have even been a "greaser" at some point in his youth.

That's right, my old man was Kenickie, without the flying car.

When the doctor plopped a wailing blob of living, breathing, soaked in vaginal goop, human flesh into his hands, I'm thinking he wished the afterbirth was his kid instead.

At least, that particular puddle of disgusting kept quiet.

Years later, when my mother told him that she wanted a divorce, the dude went bonkers. Growing up, the old man was never the most levelheaded guy. He loved to scream and he enjoyed intimidation, and he seemed to take great pleasure in removing his belt and letting loose with some *old school* parenting.

He was hard-wired for anger. It was what he'd grown up around. It was all he knew and all he was comfortable with. Some of the time, my mother was able to keep him in check and things never went too far, I guess - *although she could be a bit of a pill herself.* When she eventually flashed him the deuces and moved on to bigger and better things, the filter was gone. He was finally free to handle things *exactly* the way he wanted to handle things and he was more than ready to take the frustration he felt for his no-good wife out on his kids.

Things were about to get *awesome.*

Did I say awesome?

I meant horrible.

Sorry about that. I get those words mixed up a lot. You have no idea just how many weird situations it's gotten me into when it comes to the ol' wonka wonka .

By *wonka wonka,* I, of course, mean, huzza *wuzza wuzza.*

When I say huzza *wuzza wuzza,* I mean *bom chicka waaa waaaaa.*

In case you're unfamiliar, *bom chica waaa waaaaa* means *vodeo-do.*

If you're still confused, *vodeo-do* is essentially *fucking.*

Just how bad did things get when the judge left my brother and I in the hands of the unsuspecting bachelor? Let's hop into our H.G. Wells- inspired time machine, pull back on the old timey lever and zoom to a very specific moment in my childhood.

Why an H.G. Wells- inspired time machine? Because the DeLorean is pretty played out at this point, the box from Primer is too confusing, and I can't stand Dr. Who.

That's right nerds, I've never been able to get into the *Doctor.*

Deal with it.

A phone booth? Really? *Come on.*

The pain in my chest was unbearable. Someone was poking my lungs with a stick and tickling the nerve endings in my brain with a bigger stick. Breathing hurt and thinking about breathing hurt even more. My father looked over from the driver's seat of his mostly shitty car and wiped a bit of sweat from his forehead.

Dude was worried.

He was worried because his eldest son was clutching his chest, wincing in pain, and breathing like a female porn star on the set of her first anal gangbang who just happened to forget her tube of butt lube at home. He was worried because his kid most likely had a fractured rib and he was the one that fractured it.

Oops.

"Just tell them you fell at school."

My response was mostly garbled as that stick poking my lungs drove just a wee bit deeper. "What?"

"You heard me. Just tell them you fell at recess."

Fantastic. Now he wanted me to lie.

"When the doctor asks you what happened, tell him that you were messing around and you fell."

I didn't respond. I had other things to worry about – like the fact that the invisible man was smashing me in the chest with an invisible baseball bat and the dude had a swing like a juiced-up Sammy Sosa on a pre-game road rage.

"Are you listening to me, Steven?"

I nodded.

I was just a kid. What the hell else was I supposed to do?

Real life is a weird thing. If you think real life is anything like the movies, you're either fooling yourself or you're just a fool. You might be both.

Dude was my father. He was one of the two people in my life I was supposed to look up to more than any other. He was among the most important things in my very small world, the reflection by which I judged everything else. Dude was all I knew.

It's tough to say no to all you know, especially when your brain isn't fully formed, your balls haven't dropped, and your armpits are still as smooth as the wonderfully greased posterior of Elle MacPherson during a Swimsuit Edition photoshoot in the 80's.

Remember her? That's a Google search that'll kill an hour and tighten your britches.

When we arrived at the emergency room I told the doctors exactly what I'd been instructed to tell them.

"You just fell?"

"Yep."

"Earlier today at school?"

"Yep."

"On what?"

"A rock."

"What were you doing?"

"…spinning…"

"Spinning?"

"Yep."

"Was this in the morning or the afternoon?"

"Afternoonering."

That last bit was mostly a mumble.

It was a weird lie. I'm not entirely sure anyone truly bought it. Sometime in the *afternoonering* I'd fallen at school, somehow, onto a rock, or something, while *spinning,* and managed to fracture my rib.

It didn't really make any sense.

Then again, neither did anything else going on in my life around that time.

None of the doctors pulled me aside and none of them asked me any further questions. The guy I dealt most directly with, raised an eyebrow and threw a side-eye my way, but there's a good chance it could have just been a nervous twitch. If they bothered to question my old man, I never heard about it.

This was pretty much how things went for a couple years. Eventually, I came to my senses and moved in with my mother where I drastically improved my ability to conjure believable lies and was rarely forced to go to sleep with sticks poking my various orifices.

Just a few minutes ago I trademarked the word *afternoonering,* so don't go getting any ideas.

-Steven Novak-

MY FIRST CONCERT

MY FIRST CONCERT

When I was a kid I was also a little metal-head poseur. *Motley Crue, Poison, Cinderella, Winger, Ratt, Skid Row, Warrant,* and even the damn *Nelson* twins – I was nuts about them all. Pop-metal was the coolest thing on Earth and, from my perspective, it was never going to die.

If the band members had poufy hair, and pants so disgustingly tight you could make out the hair on their balls, I was a fan.

Let me just make it clear that I wasn't necessarily a fan *because* of the tight pants and ball hair. Let's get that straight right now and not go spreading any rumors. Seriously people, I want to make this perfectly straight - straighter than a wobbly arrow - straighter than Tom Cruise – straighter than an erect penis.

Okay, so maybe those weren't exactly the best examples.

There was a time (that I'm not too proud of) when I danced around my bedroom playing an air guitar and dreaming of, one day, being a member in a metal band. I even had a name picked out for my fictional super-group. Are you ready to hear it?

I'm warning you, it's exceptionally lame.

Seriously, it's stupid.

All right, if you really want it, here it comes - *Sleeping Beauty.*

See? I told you it was lame.

Because of my scary-sad love for all things hair band, I was, of course, overjoyed when my mother scored me some tickets to an *Aerosmith* concert.

I was going to see *Aerosmith*! I was going to see the *Black Crow*s! I was going to see *Gene Loves Jezebel!* (Which is noticeably less impressive, but still pretty cool.)

It was going to be me, it was going to be my friend, Derek, going to my very first concert!

It was going to kick ass.

Unfortunately, my mother and her boyfriend at the time, were coming along, also.

I reminded myself that, if I could deal with the presence of *Gene Loves Jezebel*, I could also deal with my mother and the guy that was mashing his genitals into her crotch as well. Though the image was admittedly horrifying, it was a small price to pay, for *Aerosmith*.

I would have done anything for *Aerosmith* - anything

Yeah, that's right, I'm looking at you, Joey Kramer.

By the time we arrived at the stadium, Derek and I were pretty amped. Neither of us had been to a concert before and we weren't entirely sure what to expect. Would we be sitting in the front row? Would we get to hang out with *Steven Tyler* and *Joe Perry* after the show? Would we become such good friends with them that they'd decide to take us along for the rest of the tour? Would we spend the next four months buried up to or necks in STD-ridden groupie-crotch?

Or maybe we'd be a sitting mile away and unable to make out anything other than *Steven Tyler's* sparkly-loud jacket?

Bingo.

Bingo on the last part, anyway. Whatever. I tried to ignore the crummy seats. It was still a concert, lawn seating or not. I wasn't going to let it ruin my day. *Love in an Elevator* would still rock. It didn't matter how far away we were and how few groupies we'd get to bang.

During the *Gene Loves Jezebel* set, I told my mother that Derek and I were going for a walk. We wanted to get away from the *adults* for a while and stretch our legs. We wanted to pretend we were alone.

My mother looked confused. "But you're going to miss *Gene Loves George,* Steven."

"I'll get over it, ma."

Derek and I ended up sitting at a table near the bathrooms and crummy souvenir stand. Not far from us, there were a couple of older girls. They were smoking and laughing, and playing with their hilariously oversized buns hair.

The way they were dressed - well, let's just say that everything was popping out.

Everything was on display. It was like a perverted, neon candy store. There were boobs. There were nipples. There was some booty and even a little booty crack. There was also some boobie crack - and some crotch crack.

Basically, anything and everything crack related was open for business.

They may have been on crack as well.

In fact, I think it's pretty likely.

Needless to say, with so much wonderful, soft, womanly parts exposed, I was finding it difficult to divert my eyes. My stare was creepy and the smile on my lips had curled into highly lecherous. All I needed to complete the ensemble was a long trench coat with nothing underneath and a bottle of Jack Daniels in a paper bag.

The taller of the two girls – and the one with the more ample bosom - noticed me ogling her through a puff of the smoke from her cigarette. I quickly looked away and turned my attention to Derek. "So, um…hey. What do you, um…what do you think about the…you know, stuff…happening, so far?"

Derek looked at me like I was crazy. "What? What are you talking about?"

I had no idea what I was talking about – none at all. In fact, I wasn't even sure who I was and where I was at. I was simply trying my damndest to cover up the fact that I was staring at the camel toe twenty feet away.

From the corner of my eye I noticed that the girls were moving in our direction.

What the hell? Why are they coming this way? Someone tell them to stop moving in our direction! Why on Earth would they feel the need to saunter over here - with their long, lanky legs – and those bouncing – jiggly jigglers – and that tightly packed cam-SNAP OUT OF IT!

My heart was racing and my mind running in circles faster than Seabiscuit, if someone was to set him on fire and let him run the track at Churchill Downs.

I needed to get away.

I grabbed Derek by the shirt and started to pull him from the table. Unfortunately, the girls were already on us. The blond one with the chest for days was standing above me, looking down at me with her glassy blue eyes and a cigarette dangling between her fingers. I noticed how much taller she was than me. For the briefest of moments, I imagined myself resting my head on the pillow of her cleavage.

I bet they were soft. I bet I would have had wonderful dreams.

She smiled at me in a weirdly sexual, just a little bit gross, completely exciting sort of way. "Hey, kid."

My voice cracked and I mumbled something that kind of sounded like words, and kind of like a teenage girl getting felt up for the first time.

As expected, she laughed. "See something you like?"

Now how the hell was I supposed to answer that?

I mean, what's the proper protocol in a sitaOUUUUUUUCCCCHHHHHHHHH!

There was a sharp pain in my leg! I jumped backward and glanced in the direction of the awful sensation. The blond girl's friend was crouched at my side with a lighter in her hand. She was laughing her ass off.

She was also trying to burn the hair off my leg.

Aerosmith sucked that night.

Plus, I had to explain the burn marks on my leg to my mother.

When she threatened to "find the girl and give her a piece of her mind," I wanted to curl into a ball and die.

When she made good on her threat later that evening, I wanted to jump off a bridge.

I never went to another concert again.

On top of it all, Pop-Metal didn't even make it out of the 80's – which made my *Gene Loves Jezebel* shirt look stupider than ever.

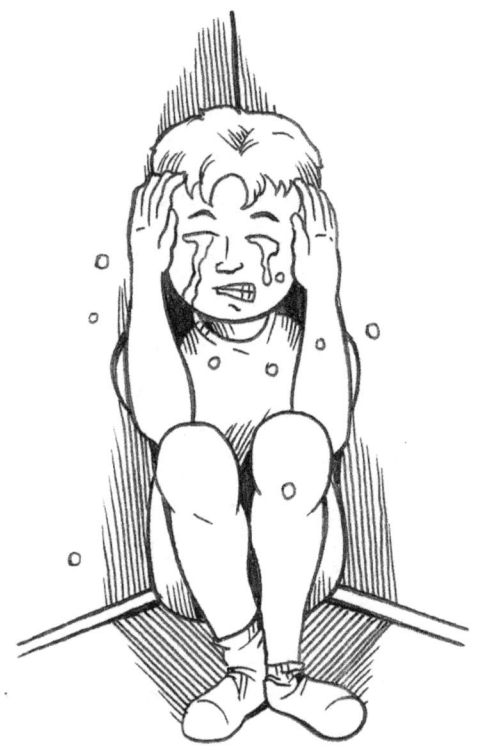

THE HORROS OF THIN WALLS

THE HORRORS OF THIN WALLS

When I was ten-years-old, my parents got divorced. I know, boo-fucking-hoo, right?

Actually, it wasn't all that negative a thing. My parents hated each other and I hated them when they hated each other. All they did was fight, and yell and sometimes throw shit.

Not *actual* shit, mind you – though that would have made my story a heck of a lot more interesting.

Speaking of stories, this one, in particular, isn't so much about the divorce as what happened afterward. It's about a moment I've tried to forget for a long, long time. It's about a moment that's burned itself into the gray matter of my brain, ensuring that I'd remember it until the day I die. It'll likely be my final thought, seconds before I inhale my last bit of air.

(Which will admittedly suck, because I would much rather my final thoughts be about a perky pair of boobs.)

It wasn't too soon after the divorce that my father started dating someone new. She seemed nice enough, I guess. Of course, the level of conversation between the two of us never really progressed beyond the occasional "hello," or "hi," or even a mumbled *"howzitgoin."*

She had a passable *howzitgoin,* though. I guess that's saying something, right?

Truthfully, I didn't much care.

I didn't particularly have any interest in being her friend, and I'm fairly certain she agreed with the sentiment.

Growing up, my bedroom shared a wall with my father's room. It was a thin wall. It was a really thin wall. I'm talking Laura Flynn Boyle thin and everyone knows that a thin Laura Flynn Boyle is of no use to anyone.

Actually, now that I think about it, a heavier version of Laura Flynn Boyle is of no use to anyone either.

Does anyone out there even remember Laura Flynn Boyle?

She screwed Jack Nicholson's corpse in the 1990's.

Anyway, one night I was asleep in my bed dreaming of *Voltron* and *G.I. Joe*, and trying to imagine what *Cheetara* looked like naked, when something woke me up.

"Umph. Hehe"

It was a muffle. It was a scuffle, a huffle and a muffle. It was all three of those things, and it was followed by a giggle.

I propped myself onto my elbows and listened intently, half wondering if I'd imagined it.

I heard nothing.

Damn it. In my mind, *Cheetara* was mere seconds from peeling off that cool orange bikini thing before I got distracted. I sighed deeply and returned my head to the pillow. If I tried hard enough, I thought that maybe I could slide back into the dream right where I left o...

"Umph. Hehe. Ooh."

There it was again. I didn't imagine it. What the hell?

"Umph." *Zip.* "Hehe. Haha. Umph."

What the fuck? Was it coming from my father's room?

That's when it hit me.

Oh, shit. Oh, dear God, no.

"Umph. Ung. Ah. Oh."

Oh, sweet. Jesus, Oh, Ganesha, and Buddha, and Zeus and Aphrodite, and Michael and Mallory, and Number Five - who indeed proved to be alive.

It couldn't be.

My father and his new girlfriend were screwing.

I tried to wedge my head beneath my pillow. I pulled it so tight over my head that I couldn't breathe. For a second, I worried that I might suffocate myself, but so what? Suffocation would have led to death and death would have led to an escape from the sound of my old man getting his screw tool suckled.

"Ung. Ung. Ah."

They were breathing harder. It was getting louder with every passing second and the pillow was doing little to nothing. The sounds were somehow finding the cracks in between the pillow and the bed, snaking their way underneath like dedicated little ninjas and wafting into my ears.

Damn it!

It was awful. It was worse than awful. It was wawful.

"Ah. Oh ya! Ah. Oh. Ung!"

They were grunting and they were groaning. The bed was creaking and the headboard was banging against the opposite side of the wall like the steady drumbeat of the Devil himself. The idea that my bed was sort of, kind of pressed against theirs was creeping me out. It was creeping me out big time. It was almost like we were all in one big bed, like I was engaged in the disgusting act with them.

I needed to get off the bed.

In a single movement, I rolled onto the floor and scurried across to the opposite end of the room. I wedged myself into the space between my dresser and the wall, pulled my legs to my chest, and buried my head into the crook of my knees.

Sports. I needed to think of sports. I needed to focus on anything other than the sound of my father sexing up the broad with the super-high hair in the next room over.

G.I. Joe. Yeah, the Joes would save the day.

My brain focused singularly on G.I. Joe - on *Flint,* and *Snake Eyes* and even *Shipwreck.*

Snake Eyes is a ninja.

Cobra Commander's voice is stupid.

The Transformers are robots in disguise.

The Go-Bots suck.

Thundercats are cool, though. Pantro, and Mummra the Ever Living – they're awesome.

Cheetara. Wait, no...not, Cheetara...

"UnG! AGH! YA! UNG!"

Shit! Suddenly I was picturing my father boning Cheetara!

I ran back to the bed, snatched the covers and charged across the room, once again. When I hit the closet door I threw it open, climbed inside and slammed it behind me before immediately curling into the fetal position. Even with my eyes shut tight, it wasn't dark enough. I needed it darker. I needed it to be as dark as it could get and then, even darker than that. I needed to poke my eyes out and rip my ears off.

Just when I thought I couldn't take anymore, the world went quiet.

The noises stopped. Were they done?

Oh, please let them be done.

If there was indeed a God hanging out somewhere in the clouds, I needed him to make them done. I promised to erect a church in his name. I swore to follow the scripture and the teachings to the letter! I just needed them to be done. I needed my father to be a terrible lover. I needed him to be quick on the draw.

I needed it more than I nee...

"Ung. Put it in my ass."

If I ever meet God, the first thing I am going to do is shoot him in the kneecaps.

THERE'S A DRUNKEN DINOSAUR AT THE WEDDING

THERE'S A DRUNKEN DINOSAUR AT THE WEDDING

His name is Phil, and he's my Uncle.

Basically he's a living, breathing dinosaur with a teeny-tiny brain to match.

The man's a holdover from a time long since gone, long before the invention of the wheel and even longer before some hairy bastard slammed two rocks together, got a spark and set a nearby bush ablaze.

Phil comes from a period in human history when the male of the species would drag his female counterpart around by her hair and had his way with her whenever he liked. He comes from a time when human beings used their bare feet as car engines, drank a beverage called *Cactus Cooler* and occasionally went on wacky adventures with prehistoric movie stars like *Stoney Curtis.*

Okay, maybe that last bit actually came from *The Flintstones.*

Phil is a beast. The man stands about 6'5 and weighs around 360. He's a massive man. His body is constructed of only three things: piss, vinegar, and booze. Not necessarily in that order.

When I was in junior high, a measly two years after my parents were divorced, my father was ready to get married again. Seeing that Phil is his younger brother, Phil was, of course, invited.

Everyone knew it was a mistake.

Everyone knew that inviting Phil to a party with an open bar was as huge a mistake as yet another formulaic cartoon from Seth MacFarlane.

About an hour into the reception, just how big a mistake it was, became abundantly clear.

Phil was going from table to table, smacking old women and young kids on the back of the head and screaming, "HEY TURD! GOOD'TA SEE YA'S!" A half-eaten hunk of fried chicken in one hand and a drink in the other, his breath smelled like a rotting corpse covered in Jim Beam.

His belt and cummerbund had long since come off and his pants had begun to slide south.

Being loud, boisterous, and having a good time is one thing - physically abusing the elderly, flashing a crack deeper than the Marianas Trench and copping the occasional feel on underage girls in the wedding party is something else entirely.

Phil's obnoxiousness reached its apex when he got pissed at some women for *"lookin' at him wrong,"* shoved her backward and sent her sliding across the lawn. The terrified old broad hit the ground hard. Her dress flipped up and over her head, which, in turn, gave everyone a crystal clear view of fifty-five-year-old camel toe.

Understandably, Phil's shove angered her husband and he responded by immediately getting into the big oaf's face. In no time at all, the pair were pushing and shoving and flapping their jaws like a couple of trash-talking boxers at a pre-fight press conference. My father and a few other guys in the wedding party took notice of the situation - as well as Phil's wife - who was a bit buzzed herself, and a pretty imposing figure in her own right.

Soon enough, there were six idiots in tuxedo's wrestling the snarling, booze-filled behemoth to the ground.

Once he was sedated and tagged like a gorilla in the jungle, they dragged Phil across the lawn and threw him into the camper near the fence.

Mrs. Phil joined him shortly afterward and, for a moment, things returned to normal - at least until the screaming started.

"Fuck you, bitch! Fuck you! Fucking fat ass whore! You don't know shit about me!"

"I don't know shit about you? You're a fucking, fuck-fuck, you asshole!"

Fucking fuck-fuck?

Who would have guessed someone could successfully place three *fucks* next to each other and make a sentence out of it?

"CUNT! FUCKING CUNT!"

The camper started to bounce up and down. The wheels were lifting clear off the grass as it swayed from side to side.

"I'll show you a cunt, you drunken piece of fucking shit!"

Damn, this woman liked the word fuck.

Suddenly, my father's wedding reception had become the single *bluest* Friars Roast in the history of Friars Roasts - and that includes the Mel Zets fiasco in 55'.

Something glass broke. "I'll show you, drunk! Whore!" Something metal bent and snapped in two.

The babbling was becoming more and more incoherent.

There were a couple of diesel trucks with Tourettes locked inside of the camper and they were having at it.

I turned my attention away from the shaking cuss box and noticed a group of people on the other side of the yard singing, laughing, doing the hokey pokey and turning themselves around.

Not long after that, my father was removing the garter belt. He stuck his head under the bride's dress, then came out and decided, in his infinite wisdom, to make a *stink* motion with his hand.

I looked back towards the camper – it was much more interesting.

-Steven Novak-

PİNE NEEDLES İN MY FACE

PINE NEEDLES IN MY FACE

I have an extremely important announcement to make. Are you ready? Are you sitting down? If you aren't sitting down, maybe you should be, because this is the sort of thing you really need to be sitting down for. I'm not joking. Plant your keyster, meister.

Okay, now that you're sitting down, are you ready? Are you absolutely one-hundred percent sure?

Okay then, here goes: I hate golf.

Okay, so maybe I should have left the word *important* out of the first sentence.

Maybe I should have left out the word *announcement* and the massive block of rambling text that came afterward as well. The fact that I dislike the game of golf hardly warrants any of the nonsense that followed.

Oh well, what's done is done, I suppose. Once you've killed your ex-girlfriend for cheating on you, chopped her into little pieces, strung those pieces together with some piano wire and made a little marionette out of her bloody stumps, there's really no going back, is there?

No more Friday nights at the Olive Garden for you, Cheaty McChoppedUp!

Yes, I said Olive Garden. I'm a big spender.

Anyway, the game of golf just bores the pants off me. Not literally of course – unless you count that one time.

They'll never let me on that course again.

When I was a freshman in high school, my parents took my brother and I out for an afternoon of golf. It was my very first afternoon of golf and, amazingly, I wasn't exactly pissing my pants in excitement over the whole thing. It was something to do though, so I wasn't exactly complaining either.

It was either an afternoon of golf or an afternoon locked in my bedroom staring at bikini-clad boobs in the Sports Illustrated Swimsuit issue, and occasionally licking the paper.

My tongue had been rubbed raw, anyway.

Having never played the game, my golf skills were, to put it nicely, somewhat limited. To put it not so nicely, I was pretty fucking awful. I'm talking Jessica Alba in a one woman, off Broadway performance of the Scarlett Letter awful.

Don't get me wrong, I could whack that little white ball a quarter mile, I just couldn't whack it anywhere near the hole.

Hehe. Whack it near the hole. Hehe.

My stepfather would offer up calm, tempered advise like, "Maybe you should try and take a little off your stroke. Might help you to gain a little more control."

My mother took a more straightforward approach. "STEVEN! COULD YOU PLEASE HIT THE BALL LIKE A NORMAL PERSON!"

I didn't listen to either of them.

Hole after hole, I whacked away at that little ball with the unbridled fury and sloppy innocence of a teenage boy whacking away at his lil' pants pal immediately after discovering masturbation. I don't recall what my final score was, but it's safe to assume that a young Tiger Woods didn't see me as future competition.

By the time we got to the last hole, I was fairly sick of golf in general. I was also a hotheaded little son of a bitch back then. Plus, I was hungry, and a teensy bit sleepy, and hot, and sweaty, and annoyed and ready to go home.

Needless to say, I wasn't thinking straight. "Hey, mom. I'm gonna drive the cart back up to the building. I'll meet you guys up there."

"Steven, why don't you just wait? We're almost done here. As soon as your brother hits his ball in, we can drive up together. Just wait a se..." She was talking, but I couldn't even hear her. Before she finished her sentence I was in the golf cart and I had it turned on. I just wanted the day to end. I wanted to get out of there and get home and lick myself a tongueful of those lovely, lovely boobies.

Reaching below the seat, I flipped the little reverse lever into position in order to back the cart up.

God damn golf. God damn stupid parents and their stupid golf. God damn stupid parents and their stupid golf and their stupid attempts at spending time with me rather than leaving me alone, unwanted and unloved! Who do these jerks think they are?

The teenage brain is a confusing thing, isn't it?

I glanced over my left shoulder briefly and slammed the gas with my angry, angry feet. It was at this point that everything went wrong. You see, instead of going backward, the cart shot forward like sperm from an engorged penis-tip.

In a matter of seconds an enormous pine tree swallowed me.

Branches smacked me in the face from every angle. Pine needles poked me in the eyes and the ears. A few sneaky ones managed to wedge themselves between my ass and the seat, trying desperately to worm their way into Wonka's fudge factory.

The cart came to a quick and violent stop when it slammed into the truck and sent me lurching forward. A twig jammed itself up my nostril.

Guess I didn't actually put the car in reverse.

I was cut up pretty bad. My parents ended up having to pay an insane amount of money to have the tree repaired.

I never went golfing again.

Not that my parents ever offered or anything.

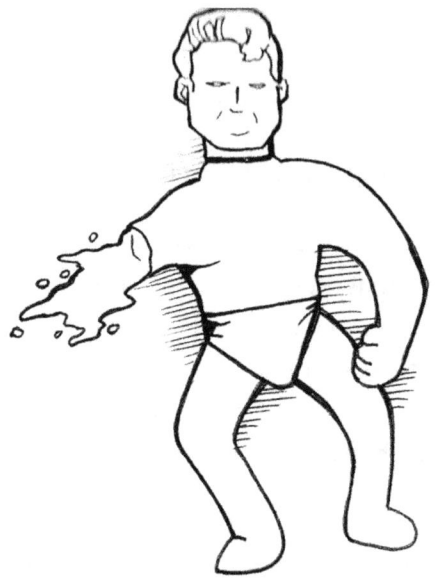

STRETCH ARMSTRONG, I HADLY KNEW YE

STRETCH ARMSTRONG, I HARDLY KNEW YE

When I was fifteen, I got my very first job. It was at a Kmart.

Why the hell they hired me, I honestly couldn't tell you.

During the interview, I was so nervous I barely formed a coherent sentence. I managed to pronounce my own last name wrong, and I dripped damn near a gallon of sweat onto the carpet of the woman tossing questions my way. Not to mention the fact that I was moments from spewing the turkey and cheddar *Lunchables* I'd eaten earlier in the day on her pretty blue shoes.

Despite all this, two weeks later I was standing behind a register in one of those swanky red vests, pretending like I gave a crap whether or not the person I was checking out had "*found everything all right.*"

"Did you find everything all right?"

"Find everything, did you?"

"Find everything you needed?"

Ug. If I'd known how to handle a gun, I might have blown my brains out.

Unfortunately, I had as much gun knowledge as Howie Mandel has comic timing, or anyone that thinks Jennifer Aniston movies are fantastic pieces of American cinema has taste.

No. I just would have shot myself in the foot. And where would I have been then?

Working the checkout line at Kmart in a cast, that's where.

No thanks, dillweed.

A couple months after starting at Kmart, my supervisor gave me a cart full of returns and told me to head into the store and put them back where they belonged. I was okay with this job. In fact, I sort of liked it. It got me away from the checkout line and it allowed me to walk aimlessly through the store pretending that I couldn't figure out where things went in a desperate attempt to kill some time.

If a shopper approached me with a question like, "*Where can I find the lug nuts?*" I'd point them in the wrong direction, then go and hide.

I knew where the lug nuts were. So why didn't I just tell them?

I dunno.

I'm a jerk? I thought it was funny? I was an idiotic fifteen-year-old and I wanted to take out the anger I felt for having to work at Kmart on innocent people? Most likely, it was a mix of all three.

Plus, let's go ahead and throw in something about my father never loving me, or some such nonsense. It works for serial killers, right? Why not me? Why should serial killers get all the breaks?

They get to eat people, they get to wear the skin of their victims as a summer dress *AND* they get to blame it all on their parents? *Screw that.* I want in on this action.

One specific afternoon, while shuffling through the store, wasting time and pointing people in the wrong direction, I found myself in the toy department. The guy who worked in Sporting Goods and the guy who worked in Electronics were huddled close near the rear of the action figure aisle. They were speaking in whispers - being real secretive and such.

Sporting Goods guy noticed me. "Hey, come here."

My *super-spy* abilities kicked in. I needed to know what they were up to and I wouldn't settle for anything less.

Bet you didn't think I had super-spy abilities, did you? Turns out, as of 2011, it's my number one ability. So suck on that.

Don't misunderstand me, I can't single handily save Air Force One from terrorists, I can't do karate or even punch a guy in the face. I can't speak fifteen different languages. I can't bed down various sexy women that are revealed to be my enemies in the last reel, either.

What I can do, and what I could do even back then, is exactly what I did: turn my head to the left and to the right to make sure no one is looking.

I never said they were "impressive" super-spy abilities.

Confident the coast was clear, I made my way over to the knuckleheads at the end of the aisle. When I was close, Sporting Goods guy motioned to one of the shelves and said, "Check this out."

Crammed in between the *Ninja Turtles Super Turtle Chopper* and some *X-Men* action figures was a Stretch Armstrong doll. Stretch was lying on his back and he had an Exacto knife protruding from his chest. He looked like the victim of a satanic cult. There was milky-clear liquid leaking from the hole in his chest cavity.

It was thick and creamy – a weird mixture of molasses and snot – sort of what I imagine Big Foot's spooge must look like.

Not that I think about that a lot or anything.

Sporting Goods guy turned to Electronics guy and offered, with a sly grin and a half-chuckle, "Dude, I totally dare you to eat it."

"No way, man. That's like…filled with toxic, and shit."

"Pussy. You don't have to eat a lot, just taste it."

"Fuck you. You taste it."

Realizing he was getting nowhere, Sporting Goods guy turned his attention to me.

Yeah, right. This idiot was even dumber than he looked, if he thought for even a second that I was going to touch the warm insides of Stretch to my tongue.

Electronics guy said it best: "it's like…filled with toxic…and shit."

I looked at Sporting Goods guy like he was insane and shook my head.

He was clearly annoyed. He was also a little angry. "Man, you two are a couple of pussies! Go to the women's section and buy yourselves some dresses, you dress- wearing pussies. Fine. I'll do it myself, but you assholes owe me like fifty bucks for doing it…each."

Nobody was going to give him fifty bucks.

Not on a Kmart salary.

Hesitantly, he touched the tip of his finger to Stretch's gooey insides, placed the glob to his lips and dabbed it with the tip of his tongue. His eyes closed. His face scrunched and his lips pulled back. Within seconds he was spitting and fanning his mouth like it was on fire. He was spinning in circles and jogging in place.

With his eyes still shut, he screamed far louder than he should have, "Aw, man! FUCK! It tastes like a ferret's pussy!"

Huh?

A ferret's pussy?

Really?

To this day I still have no idea what the hell that was supposed to mean or why he chose it as an example of something that tasted bad.

More importantly, how did he know a ferret's pussy tasted so awful to begin with?

Hell, ferret pussy might taste like cinnamon – hairy cinnamon – mixed with wood chips.

In any case, the reason Kmart hired me in the first place suddenly made complete and total sense: Look who they were comparing me to.

I WAS KIND OF A JERK WHEN I WAS A TEEN

I WAS KIND OF A JERK WHEN I WAS A TEEN

Pretty much, all teenagers are jerks, right? I mean, at least, to some extent?

Blame it on hormones, or blame it on the fact that life, as a teenager, is mostly a pain in the ass to begin with. Heck, blame it on the black guy who did all the weird sound effects in the Police Academy movies, I don't care.

No matter the reason, the fact remains; teenagers are a bunch of annoying, moody, stinky, thinking they are far more important than they really are, pains in the keyster.

Though I'd love to tell you otherwise, I was no exception.

My mother would ask me to clean my room, and, of course, I'd bitch.

She'd ask me to take out the trash, and, again, I'd bitch.

She would ask me to snap out of my emo, Nine Inch Nails and Nirvana-induced funk and cheer up, and my response would always be the same, "You don't understand anything!"

Now that I think about it, why were/are guys like Kurt Kobain and Trent Reznor always so sad? Are their lives really that tough? They had money, they had women, they had mansions, and sex with multiple partners on beds constructed entirely of hundred dollar bills. Sure, the paparazzi bugged them every once in a while. So what?

There's a kid in Africa that would chop off his toe for a sandwich. Literally. Maybe. I think. It's possible, anyway.

Stop your moaning.

How much of a jerk was I when I was a kid?

Here's an example.

"Steven, I need you to mow the grass for me."

That was my mother. She was standing in the doorway to my bedroom with one arm leaning against the frame and she was giving me the old, "*I squeezed you out of my crotch, the least you can do is help me out once in a while look.*"

I hate that look. Everyone hates that fucking look - except moms, of course. They love that look. That's the look that gets shit done.

"I'm kind of in the middle of something, mom."

It was a lie. I wasn't in the middle of anything. Unless, of course, you happen to consider occasionally giving my man parts a tug over my denim jeans while thinking of the girl in Biology with the enormous chest to be *something*.

I don't. But you might.

The truth is that I was fifteen, and I was a lazy sack of crap with absolutely no interest in mowing the lawn or doing anything remotely productive with my not so precious time.

"You can finish whatever you're working on later, Steven. I need to you mow the lawn. Don't talk back. Just get out there and do it."

Deep inside my body, the teenage male hormones took off their jackets. They cracked their knuckles and put up their dukes. Male hormones are ornery sons of bitches to begin with. They're filthy and have hair growing from odd places. They spin around in circles a lot, an almost constant tent pole in their pants as they punch at pretty much anything stupid enough to get in their way.

Most importantly, they don't like to be bothered.

My mother had riled them up and they were ready for action.

"God damn it, mom! Can't you even leave me alone for one damn minute? Why do you always have to be on me about something!"

"Oh, no you don't! Don't you ever raise your voice at me, mister! You get out there right now and mow that grass!"

"Fine! Whatever. I'll tell you what, though, I'm not doing a good job."

I stormed out of the house with my fists clenched and my face as red as a used tampon during a month of heavy flow. There was steam pouring from my ears and my teeth had locked tight.

I grabbed the lawn mower from the garage and hauled it into the backyard, mumbling to myself the entire way. "Goddamnstupidasshole…I'll show her. I'll show her about mowing lawns. StupidjerkmakingmemowwhenIdon'twanttomow…I'll teach her some lawn."

Teach her some lawn?

Yeah, I know it doesn't make a whole lot of sense. Honestly, though, very little that comes to life in a teenage brain and spews from a teenage mouth does.

After angrily starting the mower, I began to literally sprint from one end of the yard to the other – running back and forth at full speed like an absolute moron. I was breathing heavy. There was sweat pouring from my face and soaking my shirt. I was grunting, and growling, and running, so there's a good possibility I was invisible to the naked eye.

When I say fast, I mean really *fast* - faster than The Flash giving it in the hindquarters to Quicksilver in a rare, never before seen, drawing on the desk of, Joe Quesada.

When I was done, the yard looked like crap.

It looked like it was mowed by a lobotomy patient that's also a quadruple amputee, who, maybe, has Gonorrhea, or something.

When I got back into the house, my mother was staring at me as if she'd accidentally taken home the wrong baby from the hospital. She was half mad, half annoyed and a hell of a lot confused.

When she sighed and shook her head, the gods themselves took notice.

"Steven, why do you always have to make things so difficult?"

"Because you smell."

See, I told you I was a jerk.

I wasn't particularly good at witty comebacks either.

SUCK ON THAT, COUCH GIRL!

SUCK ON THAT, COUCH GIRL!

I love art.

Art was there for me when no one else was, and it'll be there until God finally says, "*I've had just about enough of knumbskull*" and puts an end to what was, for the most part, a massive mess of an excuse for an existence.

I love art and I consider myself to be an artist - *whatever that's supposed to mean.*

While I'd give my left testicle for art, I'm going be honest with you – I don't love "artists" quite as much.

There's so much overly intellectual, pompous dickery in the art world, that it can easily get in your hair and in your eyes, and miss the intended target of your brain completely.

Now that I think of it, the art world is a lot like a money shot from a first time male porn star with exceptionally bad aim.

It's sloppy and it's annoying, and entirely uncalled for.

"What's that? Oh, so let me get this straight…just to make sure I've got it right. You're saying that this wooden plank you've gone and leaned against the wall is meant to represent the suffering of the Sudanese in Darfur?"

"Yep."

"Eat me. Better yet, bend over, drop your pants and spread your ass cheeks, because I feel like ramming a handful of Anthrax up there, you schmuck."

When I was in high school, there was a girl in my art class who painted nothing but couches.

She painted couches all day – for every project – nothing but stupid couches. Sometimes they were leather, sometimes they were love seats and sometimes they looked like something you might find in your grandma's living room. On those rare occasions she was feeling exceptionally saucy, she even painted a recliner.

She did this all year long, project after project, no matter what she was asked to do, she managed to work a couch into it.

As if high school couch girl wasn't annoying enough on her own, she also managed to convince my art teacher, Mrs. Penderson, that she was a genius.

Penderson was eating out of her lap. She was munching up those couches and loving every bit of it. She was bathing in the brush strokes naked. She was grinding her most personal of areas against the armrests.

Couch girl actually managed to convince her that the sometimes red, sometimes blue, sometimes red and blue couches had really tapped into some deep and meaningful aspect of society that had, until that very instant, been avoided by the population, at large.

Couches had become deep. Couches were emo.

I wasn't really jealous of the attention the broad was getting with her couches - even if it sounds that way. Trust me, I'm not that needy. Accolades make me uncomfortable. They always have. I really do prefer to do my business in the shadows.

Let's make it clear that when I say the word *"business,"* I don't mean business as in a *"number one or two."* Doing that kind of business in the dark, well, that's just plain creepy. I'm talking the cast of Designing Women in a naked lesbian orgy creepy - which is pretty damn creepy.

The fact that that couch seemed to have everyone fooled did annoy me a bit.

I'll admit that. I'm not ashamed of it. Misplaced praise is a frustrating thing.

It's the exact reason I want to punch Katy Perry in the face.

What do I do when I'm annoyed? I set out to put the wrong things right.

I'm just like the Crow - minus the whole dead thing, and the kick ass powers and the cool bird.

At the end of the school year, the art department had a show planned that would feature the best work from the students in all of the art classes.

Couch girl was going to be there, and so would the incredible yellow and green plaid couch painting that she'd been working on all year in her *studio*.

High school kids don't have a studio. High school kids have their mother's sewing room.

Since couch girl was bringing the heat with her plaid couch, I was going to bring a little heat of my own. Game on.

I went home, dug around in the basement and found a little black jewelry box and a plastic hand left over from Halloween a few years prior. I painted the jewelry box to look like the American flag. I stuffed the hand full of twine and tissue paper that I'd dyed red and tossed the hand inside the box.

It was beautiful. It was stupid. It was idiotic. It took me fifteen minutes to make and, most importantly, it made absolutely no sense whatsoever. It also prominently featured an American flag, which not only made it instantly political, it was also bound to piss off some overly sensitive, very bored parent.

It was perfect.

The day of the art show arrived. Everyone was setting their work up in the cafeteria after school. (Glamorous, I know.) Couch girl came up behind me as I was working to find the exact position for optimal viewing of what I was now calling, "Hand In Box."

"Hey, Steve. Is this your piece?"

"Yep."

"What is it?"

"A hand in a box."

"No, what's it supposed to mean?"

"That I put a plastic hand in a box."

Mrs. Penderson stepped in between us and looked down at my gory little hand in its American flag box. "This is yours Steven?"

"Yep."

"What do you call it?"

"Hand in box."

She stepped backward. She put her hand to her chin and looked it up and down. When she was done with that, she took it in from the left and right. At one point, she even leaned over it so she could get a view of the back. She was taking it all in, observing and analyzing every square inch of my stupid little creation like she was researching an original Monet rather than something whipped into existence by a nerdy high school kid who thinks the 70's Superfriends cartoon is the absolute cat's meow.

"What are you trying to say with this piece?"

This was it - the moment of truth. "Well, basically it's a statement on this country's shoot first, ask questions later, approach to foreign policy."

Boo-Ya!

I threw some serious hippy nonsense at her with that one!

Let's stitch together hemp, some clothing, squeeze into a pair of bell bottoms and trek into the woods like a pack of half-aware donkeys and sing protest songs while we get high and completely ignore our personal hygiene!

Down with politicians! Up with animals! Hairy genitals! Now pass the bong.

"Well, I've got to tell you, Steven...I think it's wonderful. This is really, truly, a very nice piece of work. I like seeing you branch out and try and take your work to another place. Very nicely done."

And with that, Mrs. Penderson turned to another table on the opposite end of the room. Couch girl was staring at me with her mouth wide open. Her eyebrows were scrunched and I could almost swear I saw a puff of steam shoot from her ears.

It was the same look my mother had that time she caught me masturbating to scrambled porn late one night, which also happened to be the same look I had last weekend when I walked into the bedroom and found my wife watching a "Laguna Beach" marathon on MTV.

She was disgusted, she was angry, and she wanted to rip my head off.

I threw couch girl a crooked smile and shrugged my shoulders.

Her anger was misdirected, though. She shouldn't have been mad at me. She hated the player and not the game.

Art is an amazing thing.

Human beings are great at turning amazing things into jokes.

I ended up leaving the show before any of the parents arrived. Superfriends reruns were on and I was anxious to get home. I wasn't going to miss Superfriends.

NINJA ATTACK!

NINJA ATTACK!

My mother wasn't on the market for very long after her divorce. In fact, she ended up remarrying pretty quickly. Her new guy was named Glen. Glen was a nice guy. He was a quiet guy. He was a guy with a very 1970's porno 'stache.

Which sort of made him a creepy guy as well.

At the time, he was designing office products for a company called Ingento and he made pretty decent money doing it. He treated my mother fairly well, wasn't too much of a jerk, and more importantly, and most importantly, during that time in her life, he seemed to make her happy. Overall, I had no problems with the man.

Except for the 'stache of course.

Along with Glenn, came Glenn's family. They were massive. They were massive and they were tightly knit.

I found this stranger than his mustache.

I hadn't seen a blood relative in years - since I was a kid – and, even then, I barely saw them. I sort of knew what some of my uncles on my mother's side looked like, but my opinions were based on half-remembered moments and tall tales passed down through the years. Neither of my parents really get along with their families and, because of that, I rarely saw them growing up.

You might think that sounds sad, but it really isn't. I didn't have too much of an interest in hanging out with my coke-addicted uncle, Jeff, or going bar-hopping with crazy, uncle Phil, or doing a stint in prison with any one of the career criminals for knocking over the local liquor store.

Glenn's family was different - these people are always getting together. They'd get together for Christmas, they'd pray together on Easter, cook up a massive turkey on Thanksgiving. They even had a family picnic for Arbor Day, once.

Okay, that's a lie – as far as I know, anyway.

These people were always together and always crammed into a house much too small to contain them. Early on, my brother and I became accustomed to sitting away from everyone in the back of the room to wisecrack.

The whole notion of "family" was foreign to us. It was weird and creepy. It was creepier than a 1970's porno 'stache.

We were the black sheep and we kept each other entertained - until something like this would happen. "Nicholas, can you give me a hand with this?"

That was my mother. She was calling my brother into the kitchen to help her with something and she was taking him away from me.

She was leaving me alone - with my brain.

My brain and I have never been a good combination. He's always thinking. He's always busy plotting, and planning, and imagining, and, honestly, I just want to go to sleep. My brain hates me and I hate it. That's how our relationship works.

Sitting alone, in the back of the room, staring into the sea of togetherness that was Glenn's family, my mind started to wander.

The first thing it wandered to?

Ninjas, of course.

Once the ninjas have found their way into my daydreams, all hell breaks loose.

Suddenly, every single window in my mother's house exploded. Glass was flying everywhere The women were screaming and the men joined in soon afterward, rogue shards embedded in the flesh of their faces. Before anyone could make sense of what was happening, a thick black smoke began to fill the room. Tears turned to coughs; shirts went to faces in a desperate attempt to continue breathing.

This is when the ninjas arrived.

The smoke was their cover – a common ninja trick.

They poured through the newly exploded windows like water. There were twenty, maybe thirty of them with swords drawn, whispering orders to each other in Japanese and using complex hand gestures to secure the location.

The family was surrounded.

Glenn's nephew, the one who played college football, thought he spotted an opening in the ninja defense. Relishing the opportunity to play the hero, he charged at the ninja closest to him, tacked the assassin to the ground, and tried to wrestle away his sword. Moments from ripping it from the surprised ninja's grasp, another ninja stabbed him through the back and shoved forward until the blade exited out the other side. A wad of sticky-warm blood began to spurt from his mouth and sprayed across my mother's newly tiled kitchen floor.

Glenn's older brother charged at one of the ninjas from behind, screaming at the top of his lungs from underneath his equally porn-tastic 'stache.

With a single, lightning-fast movement, the ninja removed his head from his shoulders. The decapitated dome spiraled through the air and bounced off the countertop before bouncing off the carpet and rolling underneath the Christmas tree.

With the carpet drenched in blood, a single ninja stepped forward and growled in broken English, "No one else try nothing...or you, too, suffer his fate."

The younger children crawled into their mother's arms and began to sob. The wife of my headless step-uncle could only stare at the demonic Christmas present that was her husband's decapitated dome.

As I watched the reflected Christmas lights dance in the maroon pools, I realized I needed to do something. I needed to act. I needed to do something because no one else could.

Without hesitation, I stood.

Glenn's sister grabbed my arm, squeezed tight and tried to pull me back down. "Sit down! Sit down! What are you doing? You'll get yourself killed!!"

I looked back at her with silvery-blue eyes of Alaskan stone. "I know what I'm doing."

It was a lie.

It didn't matter.

The broken English ninja noticed me, turned in my direction and tightened the grip on his sword. "Listen to the woman, boy. Her words are wise."

I offered no verbal response. My expression spoke for me. My body language left no mistaking my intentions.

The ninja's eyes narrowed. There was a heck of a lot more to me than the surface suggested. Beneath my jeans, and beyond my faded Nine Inch Nails shirt, was a master of the highest order. Though it was subtle, he nodded in my direction. He'd unknowingly stepped into a hornet's nest. He'd tugged on Superman's cape and taunted an angry dog. He and his clan were in for the fight of their lives. No doubt about it.

He motioned for his ninja's to surround me. They did.

Moments later, the battle began.

I expertly avoided the strikes of the ninja clan, while at the same time managed to use their own momentum and weapons against them. I leapt over couches and slid under tables. I rolled over countertops and swung from the chandler. All the while I was chopping ninjas in half and being doused in their blood.

One dead. Two dead. Three dead. Four dead.

I was ahead of them at every turn - moving with the swiftness of the wind and fueled with a fury of vengeance.

Five dead. Six dead. Seven dead. Eight dead.

Every square inch of the room was soaked in blood and littered with body parts. I used a section of ninja intestines as a whip and a severed leg as a club. All the while my stepfather's family gasped and shrieked and guffawed – unable to make sense of what they were seeing.

Ten dead. Eleven dead. Twelve dead.

I was navigating the fine line between brutality and beauty, transforming death into art and defying the very dictates of logi...

"Steven, it's time to open your present."

"Huh?"

My mother was standing next to me, tapping me on the shoulder. "Open your present."

There was a neatly wrapped gift sitting in my lap. Everyone was looking at me and there wasn't a single speck of blood on them. My step-uncle's head was still attached to his shoulders and he was smiling at me in his unique Wisconsin, bratwurst-faced way.

My mother nudged stiffly. "Come on, Steven. Open it. It's your turn."

When the wrapping paper was removed, I found a pair of socks.

Socks.

They weren't two-toed ninja boots – they were just ordinary, gray socks.

Ninja boots would have been cooler.

-Steven Novak-

SOME KIDS WANTED TO BE ASTRONAUTS

SOME KIDS WANTED TO BE ASTRONAUTS

I have an overactive imagination. I always have and I always will. It's what makes me mildly interesting to a very select group of people thirty-five percent of the time.

The issue is that my brain just never stops thinking. This would be fantastic, if the stuff it was thinking about was important, or relevant, or even mildly relevant.

If my brain was thinking about the cure for cancer - that would be pretty awesome. If it was thinking about world peace, or putting food in the mouths of starving children, or even ending the annoying-ass career that Jennifer Garner had, somehow, managed to create for herself, I'd be a happy, happy man – but I'm not.

When I was younger, I thought even less about those things. In fact, when I was in high school and college, there were three basic themes I would daydream about, all day, every day.

1. Ninjas, fighting and explosions.

2. Girls, sex and the possibility of girls and sex.

3. Becoming a famous movie director.

That was pretty much it.

In high school, the only thing I wanted to do was direct movies - not only direct them, but star in them, produce them, write them, and maybe even, do the score.

I had no musical talent whatsoever, but that was just a minor detail.

I wanted to win awards. I wanted to receive critical acclaim and still, somehow, manage to rake in the box office receipts. I wanted to be voted the "World's Sexiest Man," despite the fact that I was, in fact, more ugly than the ugliest guy in the school after he'd been pulled from his car and beaten with ugly sticks by the L.A. Ugly Police.

I was obsessed with the idea of writing and directing, and becoming the hottest thing in town. I thought about it so much that I even worked out the titles, stories, actors and every single detail of every movie that I would ever make. I also knew how well they did opening weekend. I knew how much the ticket sales fell off after the first week. I knew what the critics thought. I knew how well they did when they were released to DVD.

In the shower, every morning before classes, I would pretend I was working the press junket and being interviewed about my many successful films.

"So, Steve, people have really taken to this new film of yours. How do you feel about the reception it's getting from both the public and critics?"

"The response from critics and fans has been fantastic…really humbling. Honestly, though, I just do this because I love doing it. Everything else is icing on the cake, I suppose."

I was always so humble.

Besides knowing every detail of every movie and the box office numbers to boot, I'd also worked out every aspect of my personal life as a major Hollywood director, rich guy, and crotch fireman to all the fiery vaginas in need of a hose out there.

After my first two films not only managed to take top honors at Cannes, but pull in a cool three-hundred million at the box office, I played the field for a bit. I stretched my legs. I tried out the merchandise and refused to be tied down and I dipped my *Fun Dip* stick in the sensual cherry sugar of quite a few of Hollywood's leading ladies.

Okay.

I generally don't like to pause in the middle of writing a story to boast about my abilities, but come on - Fun Dip stick? You've got to give me some props for that one. You just have to. I seamlessly compared a delicious childhood favorite to intercourse. You know I deserve some props. Stop hogging the props and toss a few my way. Come on. Do it. Just a couple. Three props. You can underhand three measly props in my direction.

As expected, playing the field grew tiresome and I eventually met a girl that knocked me off my feet. We fell instantly in love and I decided to settle down.

Who was the *lucky* lady I chose to be my bride?

Fariuza Balk.

You probably have no idea who the hell that is. She's not exactly an A-lister, anymore, and she wasn't really one when she was still getting jobs. In fact, for all I know, she might work at a Dairy Queen these days.

Fariuza starred in a bunch of direct-to-video garbage in the 1990's and managed to scrape together a movie career less memorable than even Steve Guttenberg's - which is quite a feat.

If you happen to be a Guttenberg fan (which is unlikely), don't go getting your panties in a bunch. Be honest with yourself. *Short Circuit*? *Three Men and a Baby*? Come on. It is what it is. Admit it and you'll feel better.

This is about the point where my Hollywood/Fariuza fantasy gets weird. (Weirder than it is already.)

You see, I envisioned that one afternoon, while attending the premiere of one of my new movies, my wife, Fariuza, would be shot.

Yep, I said shot.

A crazy Oswald-like sniper dude on the sixth floor of a nearby building - jealous of my bank account and rugged good looks – trained his scope on me, missed and ended up killing my wife, instead.

This was the sort of thing I fantasized about – often.

Which also means this was *ideally* the way I hoped my life would turn out.

Some kids want to be astronauts, some want to be firemen or cops, and there are some who want to be sports heroes, and others just hoping to win the lottery and lay around on a beach in Fiji while a peasant girl gives them a massage.

Me? I wanted to meet a girl and ask her to become my wife just so she could be shot in front of gawking paparazzi, and teary-eyed onlookers before dying in my arms.

The word *issues*, really doesn't do me justice.

It's no wonder that my mother insisted on so much therapy.

MY COLLEGE LOVE AFFAIR WITH THE LADY IN RED

MY COLLEGE LOVE AFFAIR WITH THE LADY IN RED

I was such a sad sack of crap in high school.

You know, as opposed to a *happy* sack of crap?

Anyway, that was all going to change.

After graduating, I snagged myself a decent little scholarship to the Columbus College of Art and Design in Columbus, Ohio.

I was off to another state, where I would meet new people in a new place and have new experiences. Sure, I was an outcast in high school, but college was a chance to turn things around. I could be anyone I wanted to be. The baggage was gone and I could start over fresh. Things were going to be different. I would be a new me - a better me – a stronger, more confident me. I could be the exact version of what I'd always wanted to be and more.

I could be Super-Me.

Plus, I'd seen the movies. College was going to be awesome. I'd party all night, sleep all day and wake again, only to party some more. I'd be surrounded by so much wonderfully soft female flesh that I'd need to put on my *floaties* to keep from drowning in it.

There was going to be booze. There was going be sex. There were going to be togas, and beer, and beer bongs, and debauchery the likes of which I could scarcely imagine.

There might even be a few farm animals mixed it.

Why not?

College was about experimenting, right?

My penis would be so sore from all the action it was getting, I'd have to pass it a Dixie cup full of water as it ran by on its way to the next great conquest.

It was going to be fantastic – the absolute greatest time of my life, and I was ready for it!

As you might have already guessed, absolutely none of this happened. Not any of it. Not even the part about the togas.

Freshmen year, I found myself assigned to a room with a kid named Stewart and two other guys. Out of the three roommates the school stuck me with, Stewart was, by far and away, the most normal and likeable. The issue wasn't that he was a jerk or a pain in the ass to live with, because he wasn't. The issue was that he was a bit of a dork – just like me.

Stewart was born in the backwoods of Indiana and came from an extremely religious family. They were so religious that he not only didn't believe in evolution, *"It's just a theory, Steven,"* but he also replaced the word *fuck* with the more family friendly *fudge*.

I'm sorry, but that's just wrong.

A healthy, nineteen-year-old, male screaming, "What the fudge?"

It's weird. It's weird and it's just a little creepy.

Stewart once mentioned to me that he'd never seen the original *Planet of the Apes* movie, so I showed it to him. He hated it - mostly due to the whole evolution thing. He also hated me for showing it to him.

"Why the fudge did you show me that?"

See? Creepy.

A week after moving in with Stewart, not much in my life had changed. I was still a loser. A month after, and still nothing had changed. I wasn't swimming in lady-flesh.

Wasn't I supposed to be swimming in lady-flesh?

After two months with my new pall, Stewey, the reality of the situation was beginning to set in. There was no booze. There were no panty raids. At no point was there a lampshade on my head, and not a single drunken robot dance had materialized. Nothing was different. If anything, my life was more boring than ever.

Had the movies lied to me?

The proof was in the pudding, though. I was a weirdo and I was always going to be a weirdo. I was incapable of functioning in society. I wasn't normal. I was a dork, and I was an outsider, and it was never going to change. Hell, even in at art school – packed to the brim with outcasts and freaks - I was unable to find my niche.

The movies had, indeed, lied to me. There was no denying it.

"College is the most fun you'll ever have in your life."

"You'll do things that you'll never forget."

"You'll have moments that you'll carry with you for the rest of your life."

It was bullshit – all of it.

It was the bullshit of an absolute massive bull dropping enormous shits - shits filled with peanuts the size of golf balls.

Every Friday night, a local Columbus radio station ran a show called "John Simonz Love Songs." Basically, it was a call-in show, in which people would call in and dedicate cheesy love songs to their *significant others*. It was romantic in the absolute *laziest* way possible.

Song like "More than Words" by Extreme, and "Everything I do" by Bryan Adams, and "I Just Called to Say I Love You" by Stevie Wonder, were constants. You know, the *classics*.

Every Friday night, despite asking him repeatedly not to, and once threatening him with bodily harm, Stewart would turn this on.

There we were, in a room smaller than some walk-in closets, working at our desks, less than eight feet away, completely and totally alone as Chris Deburgh's "The Lady in Red" wafted into the room like a cool autumn breeze

My dreams of swimming through a sea of naked ladies and their naked lady parts with a pair of little yellow floaties strapped to my arms had all but disappeared.

This happened every single Friday night when I was a freshman in college – and that's not an exaggeration.

It's pathetic, I know.

Don't worry, it's okay to laugh.

You can even point, if you want to.

I understand completely.

If you feel like throwing something, all I ask is that you refrain from using rocks – at least big ones.

Rocks leave bruises.

-Steven Novak-

THE CRAZY MAN IN THE THIRD ROW

THE CRAZY MAN IN THE THIRD ROW

There are a couple things that I need to make clear about myself.

One: I rarely, if ever, talk in public and, pretty much, never in large groups of people. In fact, I tend to freak out whenever I'm in the vicinity of other human beings, in general. I clam up. I lose control of my limbs. My mouth closes quicker than a shy nun's legs. All in all, it makes for a rather pathetic sight.

Two: I don't really have any friends. I haven't in years. I suppose this might have a lot to do with the first thing I mentioned. It's difficult to meet new people and make new friends when you're only capable of communicating through a series of barks, growls and grunts.

When I was in college and home for the summer, my brother asked me if I wanted to go to a WWF *(this was the olden days and there wasn't an E)* house show in Wisconsin with him and his friends. They had an extra ticket, they had exhausted every other possibility, and they were left with me.

I wanted to say no. I really did.

The embarrassing wrestling fan that lived inside of me couldn't pass up the opportunity, though. He just couldn't. No matter how much he wanted to. Sorting out the mathematics behind the conjectured relationship between string theory and a gauge theory called $N=4$ supersymmetric, sometimes referred to as Yang-Mills, would have been easier than turning down those tickets.

I mean, come on, the seats were in the third row.

The third. Damn. Row.

Not only would I have the pleasure of getting hit with the sweat of a greased up, pot-bellied Stone Cold Steve Austin at some point during the evening, but I'd also be close enough to make out the mushroom head of the Rattlesnake's penis through his teensy tiny black shorts.

Not that I'd be looking or anything.

I'm just saying that I could have - if I wanted to - and was into that sort of thing.

Um.

Maybe I should just get back to the story.

During the drive to Milwaukee, I was quiet. I don't think I managed to formulate anything even coming close to a compete sentence. I might have mumbled something reminiscent of a Cro-Magnon man with a slab of Woolly Mammoth flesh in his mouth and the clammy boob of a well-endowed cave woman in the other. That's about it, though.

In the parking lot, on our way into the arena, on the way to the seats, and when we finally sat down - *through it all, I was silent.*

As the first couple of matches came and went - still nothing.

I was practically a mute. I was a dummy seat-filler and nothing more. I was a warm body without an idea in my head, a voice in my mouth, or a glimmer in my dead eyes.

I was as quiet as a titmouse – which is sort of fitting, because around that time I was sporting a fairly nice pair of man tits – so the comparison works on a number of levels.

It was all very pathetic.

The moment Dwayne "The Rock" Johnson came to the ring, everything changed. You see, back in the days when I watched wrestling religiously, and bought every Pay- Per- View, and even performed the moves in my basement with my brother and his pals, I hated The Rock.

When I say that I "hated" the guy, I mean it. My hate was very real. It was passionate, and it ran deep, and it was more than a little bit scary.

It didn't make an ounce of sense, but there it was.

My hate for Dwayne was the sort of hate that most sane people save for the *important* things in life, like Cancer, or murder, or rape, or social injustice, or Oprah.

I wanted "The Rock" dead.

I wanted to watch him die.

I wanted to be the one to kill him.

I have no idea why.

As the good Mr. Johnson passed by us on his way to the ring - barely twenty feet away - something evil, and scary, and weird, spurned to life deep within my belly. It very quickly moved its way into my throat, where it pooled for a moment like the calm before the storm, before erupting from my gaping maw like a volcano spewing all the feces of all the people who had ever taken a shit in the long history of shitting.

"Fuck you motherfucker! Suck my motherfucking shit, you piece of shit!"

What the hell?

Where did that come from, me?

At first, I wasn't entirely sure it was me. Had I just screamed at a guy in a Speedo playing a goofy character, pretending to hurt another guy in a Speedo playing an equally goofy character?

Hm. That was bizarre.

It was Impressionist painting bizarre. It was people who actually devoted their precious time to reading the Twilight books bizarre. It was people who paid even more money to see the Twilight films bizarre.

It was Bella Swan's lower lip biting bizarre.

Before I knew it, I was standing. I didn't want to stand, but I was standing all the same. My brother and his friends were staring at me with their mouths open and their eyes wide.

Before my brain could convince it otherwise, my mouth started to scream. "I'm going to fucking kill you! I'm going to kill your dog and rape your mother, you son of a bitch!"

Holy Toledo.

I was not only screaming, but I was waving my fist in the air with foamy spittle hanging from my chin like Cujo.

I'd gone mad.

Not only were my brother and his friends looking at me, but everyone in the general vicinity seemed confused and genuinely frightened by the foul-mouth thing I'd become. No doubt, some of them thought I was drunk, because being drunk would have made perfect sense. I wasn't drunk, though. I was sober and I was of sound mind.

I should have stopped. I should have sat down and shut the hell up. That's exactly what I needed to do. I needed to shut up and sit down.

I really nee-"I'm going to cut out your brain and eat it, and take a shit on whatever's left, Rock!"

Now everyone was staring at me - including "The Rock."

I kid you not, the man was looking right at me with an expression of total confusion on his face.

When you consider the business he's in and the audience that enjoys what it is he does, one would assume that he would have become accustomed to threats against his dog and mother often enough that it wouldn't be quite so much of a shock to him.

One would assume that, and one would assume wrong.

That was the first and last time I ever went anywhere with my brother and his friends.

Mixing myself with people just isn't a good idea.

It's about as smart an idea as downing a Pixie Stick full of Anthrax.

-Steven Novak-

I WAS A BACKYARD WRESTLER

I WAS A BACKYARD WRESTLER

"Okay, here's how we'll finish it. You come running in as Delicious Mitchell Dunn and you lay me out with the garbage can. I'll stumble backward, Snatcho El Batcho will give me the Snatch-Drop and pin me."

As far as, you, the reader is concerned, I'm guessing that made about as much sense as a drunk trying to explain the intricacies of the DADA art movement outside of a bar at three in the morning while struggling to keep down twelve beers and those three-day-old burritos he had for lunch.

To me, however, it made perfect sense.

Which is sad.

You see, when I wasn't at work, the above rambling was how I spent my summers home from college. Yep, I admit it. I, Steven C. Novak, was a backyard wrestler.

And for some reason, I still wonder why I never got laid?

My old man was right when he said I was dumber than I look.

Back then, I had a character. My character had a back-story. My character had a finishing move and my character was involved in various feuds with other characters. Over the years, my character even won a few titles. *(Not that I'm bragging.)* He also lost titles. My character was hit by garbage cans and whacked chairs and slammed drywall, and he was even walloped with a car.

Yep, you read that correctly. I intentionally had someone hit me with a car.

Let me just run that by you again, in case you didn't quite grasp the stupidity of what I was saying. You see, I willingly allowed one of my brother's friends to drive a car at me at a high rate of speed while I jumped up onto the hood and rolled off.

I did this intentionally.

I did it with a smile on my face.

I was proud of myself afterward.

What was my IQ again?

The most embarrassing thing about all of this tomfoolery was that every single second of it was filmed. Yep, we recorded it all. There are close to a hundred hours of this stuff on the shelves in my office.

Initially, it started out as a joke. When my brother was in High School he would invite his friends over to the house on Monday nights to watch *Monday Night RAW*. At some point, one of us suggested that, instead of simply watching, it might be fun to try it for ourselves.

It was the natural progression of things, right? *No?* Only if you're a loser with no real social life to speak of beyond your Friday night *"dates"* with your right hand access to the Internet?

Luckily that description fit just about everyone in the room.

Almost immediately after it was suggested, we took to the basement and wrestled our first *match*. One match led to two and two led to three. Three led to four and four led to five, and five to seven, and seven to levels of absurdity that are rarely seen outside of mental institutions and those beauty pageants that feature toddlers with super high 1980's hairdo's and crazy, obsessive moms.

On one occasion, four or five of us were in the driveway of my mother's house filming a segment that required one of the characters, played by a kid named Seth, to be thrown in the trunk of a car owned by two other characters played by a couple of schmoes named Ryan and Mark. Once Seth was in the trunk, Ryan and Mark were supposed to hop in the car and drive away.

I was given the job of working the camera.

It was supposed to be a perfectly corny, beautifully staged kidnapping - *minus the pesky amber alert, subsequent police chase, and eventual prisoner rape in jail, of course.*

Everyone put on their costumes - which were basically lame-ass Halloween masks. We moved into our positions and went over the lines one last time. As the cameraman/director, it was my job to call, "action!"

Ryan and Mark pretended to attack Seth. They pretended to punch him a couple of times and they pretended to knock him out. They pretended to pick him up and shoved him in the trunk, and slammed the door. Everything was going perfectly according to plan.

And then the pizza guy rolled up.

We froze.

None of us was sure exactly how to handle the situation.

There were two grown men - two jackasses - wearing Halloween masks in August and another grown man - also a jackass - filming them with an idiotic grin on his face.

To say that we looked stupid would be a massive understatement.

We had long since moved past simply looking stupid. Calling us *stupid* is like calling William Shatner *"a bit chubbier than he used to be."* Sure, technically it's true. However, it doesn't even come close to capturing the gravity of the situation.

The man's face looked like a piss-soaked cantaloupe that's been stung by a thousand bees these days.

As the pizza guy approached, still fidgeting with the bill, Ryan and Mark ripped off their masks and hid them behind their backs, in a desperate attempt to look *natural*.

It wasn't working.

The pizza guy took in the situation and stopped dead in his tracks. His mouth dropped open and he swallowed deeply. He looked like he'd just stumbled onto a drug deal in an alley. He wasn't sure what to do next.

For a minute or so, he just stared. "Um. I have a pizz-"

BAM! BAM! BAM!

Seth was banging on the trunk from the inside. He didn't know what was going on and he was pissed. "What the hell? Let me out!"

Now the pizza guy was staring at the trunk.

Then back at us.

Then back at the trunk.

Then at us.

I can't even begin to fathom what the poor son of a bitch must have been thinking. I can only assume that he either wanted to laugh, or throw the pizza into the air and run away screaming.

Maybe it was a combination of the two?

With Seth screaming and pounding away at the trunk, Mark walked over, unlocked it and let him out.

Seth immediately sat up, pointing and screaming and waving his hands around like a crazy man. "What the fuck, assholes? Are we doing this or aren't we? I don't want to sit in this stupid trunk all day! What's goi-" He noticed the pizza guy and instantly clammed up.

Now everyone was staring at each other and no one was saying anything.

The situation was the very definition of the term *"uncomfortable silence."*

Eventually, my mother strolled out of the house, paid the poor bastard, and sent him on his way like there wasn't anything weird, at all, going on. In fact, she didn't even acknowledge us. *In hindsight, it was probably the smartest play.*

During the entire exchange, Seth never once removed his mask. I suppose he just decided it was better to leave it on rather than let the pizza guy see his face.

It was the smartest decision any of us made that day.

THE INFERNAL COOING OF THE DEVILISH PIGEON

THE INFERNAL COOING OF THE DEVILISH PIGEON

I hate pigeons.

I hate them more than Michael Vick hates dogs.

I hate them more than fans of Michael Vick hate good taste and common sense.

I hate them more than Christians hate the devil and more than Mel Gibson hates the Jews.

I hate them more than I hate each and every movie Mel Gibson has ever made and the fact that he fooled the world into thinking *"Braveheart"* was anything other than a complete waste of unused film stock.

I hate them more than you hate the fact that I keep doing this whole *"I hate them more than"* thing.

I really hate pigeons. I can't stress this enough.

I first experienced the annoying creatures born of Satan's rectum, more commonly known as the pigeon, around the time I moved to Columbus, Ohio. I was in college at the time and I'd just moved into my very first apartment in the heart of the city. It was a tiny little box - and not the good kind that you stick your penis into. *(Get it? Tiny box? Penis? Eh. It sounded funnier in my head.)*

Basically the apartment was little more than a bathroom attached to a bedroom / living room / office / kitchen / television / masturbation area. It only cost me three hundred bucks a month, and, most importantly, it allowed me to live off campus. I had spent my freshman year dealing with annoying roommates and I wanted, very badly, to live alone.

If I had been forced to co-exist in a tightly packed space *(not the kind you stick your penis into)* with another roommate, someone would have died.

I needed to live alone.

The very first morning, after my very first night in my very first apartment, I was awoken at six in the morning by an unfamiliar sound coming from just outside my window.

"cooo…cooo…cooo…cooo…"

What the hell?

"cooo…cooo…cooo…cooo…"

It was a fucking pigeon, and it was the first I'd heard outside of a television show or a movie. I rolled over. I wedged my head underneath the pillow and tried my damndest to go back to sleep. I failed.

"cooo…cooo…cooo…cooo…"

Son of a bitch.

The damn thing refused to shut up. It cooed and it cooed and it refused to stop cooing. I spent the morning tossing and turning, and sleeping for no longer than five minutes at a time, until I finally gave up and decided to simply remain awake.

It cooed through my shower. It cooed through my breakfast. It stopped cooing just as I was leaving for class.

Bastard.

The next morning it was back.

"cooo...cooo...cooo...cooo..."

You've got to be kidding me.

"cooo...cooo...cooo...cooo..."

I'd had enough. I wasn't going to let some disease-infested bird ruin my new life, in my new apartment. I needed to be proactive. I needed to solve the problem, rather than waiting for it to solve itself! I crawled over to window and bashed my fist against it a few times. The little jerk immediately flew away.

Ten minutes later, "cooo...cooo...cooo...cooo..."

He was messing with me.

He really had flown from Satan's rectum.

"cooo...cooo...cooo...cooo..."

I wanted to kill this bird.

"cooo...cooo...cooo...cooo..."

I wanted to kill his family too. I wanted to find his pigeon wife and ring her little pigeon neck. I wanted to hunt down her newly laid eggs, snatch them from the nest, fry them up and enjoy their scrambled baby embryos.

"cooo...cooo...cooo...cooo..."

The feathery piece of crap was taunting me. He knew exactly what he was doing, and I knew that he knew that I knew exactly what he was doing. It went on like this for nearly a week – back and forth we clashed – him cooing and me punching the window and cursing under my breath. My knuckles were sore and I was delirious from lack of sleep.

Wednesday rolled around and the cooing hadn't stopped. It was morning, and the *jerk* was at it again.

I crawled to the window half asleep and fully pissed off. I stuck my hand through my drawn blinds, and started frantically turning the little lever that moved the mechanical arm that closed my window. Once it was closed, the cooing stopped. I went to sleep.

The next morning there was no cooing at all. The following morning was the same. Things went on like this for a week.

Maybe the little asshole had finally moved on? Maybe he died? *(Oh, how I wanted him dead.)* Maybe he was captured and eaten by a desperately hungry hobo? *(Oh, that would have been even better.)*

Honestly, I couldn't have cared why he'd chosen to suddenly leave me alone. All that mattered was, that he was gone – and he was gone – and I was elated.

Don't look a gift horse in the mouth. That's what my momma taught me. She also taught me that *it only hurts the first time.* Or, no, wait. That was what Darnell taught me in prison.

After two blissful weeks of wonderful, sleep filled, pigeon-free mornings, I walked over to my window and opened up the blinds.

There, smashed between the glass and the screen was a dead pigeon.

Ew.

Apparently, when I closed the window two weeks ago, the little idiot got caught in the middle. I never even noticed. I suppose I should have felt bad for my feathery foe and his unceremonious demise, but honestly, I didn't.

Actually, sleeping had been far too fun. Plus, when he was alive, the dude was sort of a douche bag.

Reaching over, I cranked the lever that moved the mechanical arm, and opened my window. Unfortunately, his smashed corpse didn't move. He was plastered to the screen like he'd been stuck there with crazy glue, his head bent backward and his beak stuck in the mesh of the screen.

I did the only thing I could do: I gave the screen a slap, and sent his carcass falling four stories to the sidewalk below.

His wafer-thin body caught the breeze and floated for a moment before landing about five feet from a guy in a dark blue suit. The crumply carcass from above caught Mr. BlueSuit off guard and he leapt into the air as if someone had goosed him in the ass.

It was kind of gross – and a bit sad, I guess.

You know, in a very, very funny, sort of way.

It also made me hungry for breakfast - eggs and pancakes.

Delicious.

THE DAVE THOMAS BATH

THE DAVE THOMAS BATH

Sophomore year of college I moved out of the dorms and got myself a tiny studio apartment in the heart of downtown Columbus, Ohio. The rent was $300 a month, it smelled like the rent was $300 a month and I occasionally spent my night spooning a cockroach or two. None of that mattered, though.

What did matter was that I was finally living on my own. I was living on my own, I was living in the city, and I had absolutely no one to answer to. I could make as much noise as I wanted to make. I could clean when I wanted to clean and I could fart when I wanted to fart.

Hell, I could've bought myself a bearskin rug, stripped naked and rolled around on it while masturbating and listening to The Macarena, if I'd wanted to.

Not that I wanted to.

Cause I didn't.

The Macarena was popular at the time.

Don't judge me.

I was excited about the idea of finally being on my own and doing my own thing, and being my own man. It was going to be fantastic! It was going to kick ass! It was going to soak the first round of ass kicking in alcohol and slap on a few band-aids to allow the ass kicking wounds to heal. After that, it was going to kick ass again! I was pumped! I was ready to go!

Let's do this shit!

Truthfully, I should have known better than to be so excited.

Excitement has never worked out for me.

Fast-forward to a month or two after I'd moved in. I woke up in the middle of the night and my head was pounding harder than Chris Brown pounds his ladies and Mel Gibson pounds back the booze.

Even though it was a particularly chilly night, I was covered in sweat. My hair, the sheets, my pillow, everything was soaked. Everything was sticking to me. My bed and my body were drenched in a disgusting, sort of clear and sort of piss-colored moisture.

The room smelled like the armpits of John Belushi's corpse – or the armpits of Jim Belushi's career – or the armpits of Jim Belushi's armpits.

My body was on fire and my head was cloudy. There was a mean-spirited gymnast sporting a pair of spiked golf shoes and doing a floor routine in my stomach. There was a mariachi band worming their way through my intestines and a layer of magma boiling just inside the crinkled exterior of my anus.

It was hot. *Oh, damn, was it hot.*

My head weighed a thousand pounds.

Things were getting blurry.

I needed to lower my body temperature. I needed to lower my body temperature quickly, and I needed to lower it before my insides became my outsides. There was no time to actually check how high my fever was – no time to think - *I needed to lower my body temperature.*

After rolling from the bed, I crawled across the floor and into the bathroom, leaving a trail of slippery sweat behind. While sliding awkwardly across the hardwood on my river of perspiration, I recalled something my mother once told me about the first couple years of my life.

You see, as a child I was constantly coming down with fevers. These weren't little *girly* fevers either. These were 104 or 105 degree fevers. These were the kind of fevers that could grill steak and sauté brains. When this happened, apparently, my mother would have to strip me down, wrap me in cold blankets and lay me on the kitchen table.

I didn't have enough blankets. I didn't even really have a table.

I had ten empty pizza boxes.

That wasn't going to work, though.

I needed to lower my body temperature.

Grunting the entire way, I lugged my drippy, sweat-drenched flesh to the bathroom, leaned into the tub and filled it with ice-cold water. It took some squirming to get rid of my clothes, but I did exactly that.

My penis was going to shrink to toddler size the minute I climbed into that thing, but it was unavoidable.

I tossed a military salute in the direction of my dong and offered up a remorseful "Godspeed."

A part of me actually expected it to answer back.

My temperature must have been off the charts because I obviously wasn't thinking straight.

After five minutes in the icy drink, I was starting to feel a bit better. It was working. Sure, certain appendages were getting frostbitten and there was a good chance that I might lose a toe or two, but, whatever. Appendages could be surgically replaced and toes were useless, anyway. At least I didn't feel like I was taking a vacation on the surface of the sun anymore.

Just when I thought things were getting better, they got significantly worse – because that's the way things work for me.

Things are jerks.

Suddenly something was alive in my stomach. There was something evil in there - something big and hairy, and nasty and scary, and something with two tickets for the ferry. *(Rhyming is fun.)*

Whatever it was, it had already devoured the gymnast in the golf shoes, and it was climbing in the direction of my mouth with bad intentions.

I jerked forward so wildly you'd have thought I was possessed by a demon. My body lurched, then recoiled, and lurched again. For an encore, it convulsed.

Chunks of something that sort of, kind of, sort of resembled the Wendy's double cheeseburger I'd eaten earlier in the day began spilling from my mouth like diarrhea from the fiery-hot backside of a Schnauzer. There was bread, and there was beefy leather boot, and there were salty grease fries, and they were all mashed together, sticky with noxious bile.

SPLASHsPloooNNkkkkkplop!

That's what it sounded like.

A never-ending torrent of the foulest mouth gunk in the history of mouth gunk was splashing into the water around me – plopping and expanding, and melding with my icy surroundings.

This was what the hail looks like in hell.

For nearly five minutes, I continued to spew and gag and reload, only to spew some more. My throat was raw. My eyes were red and my face salty with tears. I couldn't breathe and I honestly didn't want to breathe. I wanted to die. I wanted to close my eyes and never wake up. I wanted to remain exactly where I was – floating in a chilly tub of my own insides.

Like an Eskimo after a really good shit followed by a really good screw, I was frozen, I was naked and I was empty, and I was spent.

Thirty or forty minutes later *(time had lost all meaning at that point)*, I somehow managed to roll out of the tub, get myself dressed and walk a few blocks to the hospital down the road.

For two days afterward, the stench of my Dave Thomas bath stuck to me like honey to a Pooh Bear.

The doctor told me it was probably food poisoning.

I told him my old pal, Dave, would never do that to me. Dave loved me and we'd been through a lot together.

He told me I was an idiot.

-Steven Novak-

MR. MOVIES

MR. MOVIES

To say that I was a bit of a loner in college is sort of like saying Nicholas Cage is just a *little* bonkers and George Clooney is *sort of* a poon hound.

The truth is that Nic drinks goat blood and sleeps in beds of ejaculate-stained first editions of Spider-Man#1 while Clooney has used his dong to take the vaginal temperatures of every broad in the 90210 area code.

Vaginal temperatures. Heh. That made me laugh when I typed it.

For three years I lived alone, and for three years I left my cramped 10x10 closet of an apartment long enough to attend classes, occasionally grab a burger from the Wendy's down the street, and return home.

I didn't talk to anyone, I didn't look anyone in the eye, and I certainly didn't invite anyone over to chat about the scholastic haps.

No one would have come, anyway – mostly because I had a tendency to use phrases like *scholastic haps*.

Back then, I didn't have Cable and I barely had the Internet. When I wasn't working I was staring at the walls in silence, and when I wasn't staring at the walls in silence, I was masturbating while staring at the walls and occasionally grunting.

When I was done masturbating, I would usually cry.

GOOOOOOO COLLEEEEGGGGEEE!

With no television and a sore penis from my furious tear-filled jerk sessions, I needed something else to distract me from my sad excuse for a *life*.

I found that distraction in movies.

Literally out the back door of my apartment building and across an alleyway was the Columbus Metropolitan Library. Unlike pretty much everything else in the city of Columbus, the library was a place worth visiting.

Also unlike everything else in downtown Columbus, it didn't smell like forgotten dreams and hobo creams.

Hobo creams. Heh. I'm on a roll.

The place was massive. It was an absolute wonderland of information spread across three floors and square footage, of which I'm too lazy to do the math. A person could get lost in there. Sometimes, on the weekends, they would pack entire orchestras into the main hall and have them spend the day playing. There were gift shops and coffee bars. These were chandeliers and there were authors coming for visits on the regular.

Not that I bothered to attend any of them.

I was too busy masturbating and crying.

There were even partitions between the urinals in the men's room.

That's hoity-toity upscale livin' where I come from.

The third floor of the library was dedicated to *"new media."* Keep in mind that this was back in the late 1990's and *"new media"* in the late 1990's was basically books on CD, those darn new-fangled *confusers* everyone was talking about, and, of course, VHS tapes.

The collection of VHS movies was, in a word, fanfuckingtastic. Anyone with a library card was allowed to check out three flicks at a time. The day the movies were returned, three more could be checked out. It was completely free, there weren't any limits on how many could be checked out in a week, and while I didn't have Cable, I did have a VHS player.

It was perfect.

I had no friends. I had no Cable . I had nowhere else to be. I had all the time in the world on my hands and I had a treasure-trove of free entertainment at my disposal.

At first, things were great. I was seeing movies I'd never seen. I was introduced to Kurosawa and getting to know Jean-Luc Goddard, and becoming reacquainted with Alfred Hitchcock. I saw *The 400 Blows* for the first time. I snagged myself a copy of *The Pawnbroker* and finally got to see Kubrick's *Paths of Glory*. I was falling in love with cinema in a whole new way and I was masturbating a heck of a lot less.

Strangely enough, I was crying more, but it was a very different sort of cry.

After a month of almost daily movie runs, things started to get weird.

"Back again? Wow."

"Weren't you just here yesterday?"

"You again! You must really love movies."

Ug.

"What's on the plate for today, Mr. Movies?"

Damn it.

The employees had become accustomed to my face. They were seeing me every day and they were remembering me with their stupid brains. Suddenly, they wanted to chit-chit. I was the weirdo they talked about during their lunch break. I was the creepy guy in the trench coat checking out three creepy movies they'd never heard of, almost every day. I was becoming a mascot.

I was Mr. Movies.

I didn't want to be Mr. Movies.

The moniker didn't do anything for my already fragile ego, and it certainly wasn't going to do anything for my non-existent love life. I wanted to be Mr. Big Dong, or Mr. Fat Wallet. Even Mr. Nowak. I wouldn't have even cared that it wasn't even my name. *Why couldn't they just call me Mr. Nowak?*

Mr. Movies was 78th on the list of the 100 Misters I wanted to be known as – right before Mr. Punches babies and right after Mr. Mxyzptlk.

In order to avoid their awkward glances and comments and the pitied looks on their faces, I took the time to learn the schedules of everyone working in that section. I knew who would be there in the morning and in the night and on what day of the week. I planned my trips accordingly.

Three times a week – that was my goal. I didn't want to run into any of them more than three times a week. Nine artsy, and sometimes not so artsy VHS films a week was still monumentally sad, but it wasn't nearly as sad as twenty-one.

For a little while, this worked.

"Haven't seen you around here lately."

"Where have you been?"

"What'cha been up to, Mr. Nowak?"

Fug. Well, it was working for the most part.

In any case, I wasn't Mr. Movies anymore. I'd beaten the system. I'd outsmarted the library employees and I'd tricked them into looking at me exactly the same as they did every other pathetic, no-life sap that strolled into the place looking for the absolute cheapest of cheap entertainment.

With my chest puffed, my back straight, my chin held high and three VHS movies tucked under my arm, I headed to the local Wendy's to celebrate victory with my traditional double cheeseburger, medium fries and a coke.

The moment I arrived, the woman behind the counter spotted me and screamed from across the room, "Hey, burger baby! I'll have your order ready by the time you get to the front of the line, honey!"

From Mr. Movies to Burger baby.

I really needed to find new places to hang out.

-Steven Novak-

UNEXPECTED VISIT

UNEXPECTED VISIT

By the time I was a junior in college, I had pretty much all but removed myself from the outside world. I was paying three hundred dollars a month for a studio apartment in Columbus, Ohio, and besides the time I spent in classes, I almost never left it.

The outside world was terrifying.

I never opened the blinds. I had no Cable or Internet. I rarely ate. And most importantly, I hadn't said a word to another human being in months. My days consisted of sitting silently in my apartment, drawing pictures, listening to depressing music, occasionally masturbating and, of course, dealing with the overwhelming feeling of sadness that would undoubtedly settle in post-jerk session.

Whoo-Hoo! College! Partyyyyyy!

Removing myself from the world at large, meant that I was spending way too much time inside my head. *That's never a good thing for anyone.* I was sinking deeper into myself, with each passing day, and the depression quickly became unbearable.

It was around this time that I started cutting myself.

Note: I have tried my damnedest to find the *comedy* in each and every story in this book, even when the subject matter didn't naturally lend itself to hijinks and mirth. Some are tougher than others and I wasn't always successful.

Let me just tell you this; self-mutilation, this is going to be one of those rough ones.

If I can do it, I really think I expect some sort of prize. New shoes, maybe? How about a pizza? *I love a good pizza.* Wait, I've got it - a new exacto knife? My old one is coated in dried blood. It doesn't cut as smoothly as it used to.

So anyway, self-mutilation. How the hell did I get to that point? I have no idea.

An exacto knife and skin - seeing them separately doesn't necessarily make the average person think that they go together like peanut butter and jelly, or Kermit and Miss Piggy. Then, again, I'm not sure if I've ever been referred to as an *"average person."*

I'm far dumber.

My self-mutilation adventure began one afternoon when I decided to carve the word *"dead"* into my right bicep.

Wait, wait, I'm not done.

After carving the word into my flesh, I rubbed a bottle of black artist's ink into the wound. It wasn't exactly hygienic and it wasn't exactly the method they teach in tattooing school, but it was the route I chose.

Once again, let me reiterate just how dumb I actually am.

For two weeks afterward, I walked around with a bright red, puss-covered, puffy, infected arm. I also wore short sleeve shirts in order to show it off – *which didn't help the "friend" situation any.*

It was during this period that I began hanging up reminders of how pathetic I was all over my apartment walls.

"Loser."

"Pathetic."

"Kill Yourself."

"You're worthless."

"Britney Spears made more money last year than you will ever make in your life."

That last one hurt more than the arm carving.

There were at least 100 of these things plastered around my apartment. Most were variations on the established theme - you know, the "*Steven sucks theme.*"

I believe it dates back to the Renaissance period, but I could be wrong on that.

Maybe Baroque?

Each of the sayings was scrawled in dark black ink, with a large brush on an 11x17 sheet paper. They were massive, and they covered the walls completely. There were so many of them that they became my own personal, depressing, weird emo-kid wallpaper.

Not exactly the kind of stuff you'd find showcased on the Home and Garden channel, but certainly a conversation starter.

After months and months of sweating, and stewing, and soaking in my personal den of depression like a slow-cooked pot roast, there was a knock on my door.

KNOCK. KNOCK. KNOCK.

Huh?

What the hell?

Who the shit?

I couldn't figure out why someone was knocking on my door. No one ever knocked on my door. My door was untouched. It was a knock virgin and it's hymen had just been ripped.

I lumbered over to the door like the troll I'd become, closed one eye and looked through the peephole. It was Stewart. Stewart was my roommate from freshman year. I hadn't talked to Stewart in a very long time, and, suddenly, he was standing outside my apartment, knocking on my door.

The nerve. The gall. *The buttered scones on this kid.* Where did he get off? Why was he there? How did he even know where I lived? No one invited him! Couldn't he understand that I wanted to be left alone? Wasn't the fact that I hadn't contacted him in a year a hint of that very point?

I had flesh to cut and depression wallpaper to hang!

He knocked again and against my better judgment, I opened the door. "Hey, Stew." I looked like hell. I looked like Jeffery Dahmer's Thanksgiving dinner.

"Hey."

We stood there for nearly a minute, staring at each other in silence, and not saying a word. I think he expected me to invite him in and maybe offer him a drink. I really believe that he wanted to sit down and talk about old times, or something.

That wasn't going to happen.

Eventually, I broke the silence. "So, what do you need?"

"Just came to see how you were doing. I pass by your place all the time. I can see your apartment from the street. It's easy to tell which one is yours…the blinds are always closed."

Funny guy - a clown, this one. He was missing his big red nose, though. A very real part of me wanted to punch him in the face and help him out with that.

Wait, no. I didn't mean that.

Stewart was a good guy. I didn't really want to punch him in the face. I'd just forgotten how to relate to other human beings.

I still didn't want to invite him in, though. I didn't want him to see just how far I'd sunk.

Or did I?

Surprisingly, another part of me wanted to invite him in. I felt like I needed to let someone – *anyone* - see just how far I had sunk. Plus, it might have scared the piss out of him. Which would have been funny.

The second part pulled an Uzi and blasted the first part away, leaving blood and chunks of flesh splattered across all my sad-guy wallpaper.

Stewart got invited in.

The minute after he stepped into my apartment and took one look around, he stopped dead in his tracks. His eyes moved from filth on the floor to the awkwardly scribbled "dead" on my arm, to the crazy-person ramblings on the wall and the dead cat hanging in the kitchen.

That's a lie. There wasn't a dead cat hanging in the kitchen.

It was actually in a pot of stew on the stove.

I could literally hear Stewart swallow. His breath quickened. He'd just stepped into the house from the Texas Chainsaw Massacre and he wasn't entirely sure how to react.

In any case, he very much regretted ever stopping by, and I could tell that he wanted to turn around and run. He wanted to run and keep running until he got back to his own apartment, slammed the door and latched it shut.

Stewart turned very slowly and looked at me with unblinking eyes. "So, um. Hey, what'cha' been up to? Haven't seen you…around…for a while. Been…um. Keeping busy?"

I scratched my head with my knuckles. "Yeah, sort of. Lots of school work." I scratched my balls with my forearm.

"Yeah, I've been busy myself. Um, hey…what happened to your arm?"

What the hell was I supposed to say to that? He pretty much knew what happened to my arm. It was obvious. There was a damn word carved into my flesh.

In response to his stupid question, I offered an equally stupid answer. "I cut it shaving."

When he took a step backward, I took one forward.

Then I scratched my ass with my shoulder.

Stewart didn't stick around very long after that. In fact, he was out the door and running home within the next five minutes.

This was the first and last time my former roommate decided to stop by my apartment unannounced.

It might have been the first time he'd pissed his pants as an adult, however.

FIRST IMPRESSIONS

FIRST IMPRESSIONS

"Steven, if Glen's family starts talking to you about religion or anything like that, you need to just nod your head and agree with them, okay?" This is what my mother said to me minutes before the first time I met my stepfather's family, years ago.

"Steven, what are you planning on saying as a toast at your brother's wedding? Because, you know, maybe you shouldn't just say the first thing that pops into your head. No one wants to hear that." This is what my mother said to me a few months before my brother's wedding, at which I was called on to deliver a toast.

"Just shut the fuck up, dummy." This is pretty much what my father said to me, all the time.

You see, sometimes I'm a little too honest for my own good.

Honesty is a fantastic quality to possess, don't get me wrong. I mean, they didn't call Lincoln "Honest Abe" for nothing, right? How wrong can it be to be compared to Abraham Lincoln?

Parents across the world spend years attempting to instill an honest nature into their children at the earliest of development. Honesty is something to aspire to. Honesty is something to be admired and respected. Honesty will get you into heaven and all that jazz.

While all of that may be true, it's not *completely* true.

The truth is that there's a time and a place for honesty, but there is also a need for outright lies.

Shutting the hell up is pretty important too.

You'd think that, after thirty years on this mud ball we call Earth, I would have figured out where and when to use all three of those options. I haven't though.

Maybe it's because I have an extra thick skull? Maybe it has something to do with the fact that I'm a slow learner? Maybe it's because I'm just plain stupid?

Sometimes I'm as dense as a dying star and sometimes I'm even denser than that. Sometimes I'm as dense as Kim Kardashian's rump meat.

I honestly have no idea what my problem is. I suppose a part of me actually thinks my blunt honesty is sort of whimsical in a way. It's fresh and it's unique, and it's, maybe even, a little endearing to some.

Or not.

I dunno.

I think most people just think I'm a douche bag.

Whimsical sounds so much better, though, *so I'm going with whimsical.*

It's not that I'm an asshole – please don't just assume that I'm an asshole. And it's certainly not that I hate every person walking the planet – because I actually only hate about three fourths of them. *It's just the way I am.*

Rest assured, that for every one, terrible thing I say about someone else, I will likely say ten things, even worse, about myself.

I'm weird.

No, um. I mean whimsical. I'm the whimsical king of creating uncomfortable situations by divulging too much information.

That's me, Mr. Whimsical.

A while back, a friend of my wife's was blabbering on and on about her little poop-bag kid, "Well Steve, don't you think our little Ashlee is the most precious thing? Seriously. Have you ever seen anything like her?"

I responded with, "I guess, sure. It looks like she's pooped her pants though. That's not really what I would call precious."

Another time my wife asked me what I thought of her red and white plaid gaucho pants, "Well, how do these look?"

I answered the only way I knew how, "Kick ass...if you happen to be a circus performer."

One of the only times a girl ever gave me the slightest bit of attention in college occurred when she said to me, "Hi. I just wanted to tell you that I really loved the painting you were working on in class today."

As suave as ever, I responded with, "What? You're nuts. Come on. We both know it sucked. I've taken shits that were more compositionally pleasing that than heap."

Needless to say, she didn't ask me if I wanted to get a cup of coffee.

Then there was the very first time I met my wife's mother. I'd just moved across the country to live with my blushing bride when her mother decided to come down from the bong-soaked, hippy-stank part of the country known as Northern California for a visit. The three of us were sitting around in the living room, less than half an hour after she arrived, and chatting about mostly meaningless nonsense. I'm not entirely sure how the conversation veered off onto the nature of good and evil, but it did.

My wife's mother, who really is a wonderful woman – even if she has something against shaving her armpits – chimed in with, "I like the idea of good and evil being black and white. There is something so pure about absolute good and absolute evil. You either do the right things, or you don't. It's simple, and it's a beautiful concept. It makes sense."

I tried to bite my tongue. I should have just bitten my tongue. It was a stupid conversation anyway, and it wasn't worth not biting my tongue about.

I just couldn't.

I mean, come on. Black and white? Life is black and white? *Seriously?* That's just silly.

It was an unimportant, completely forgettable conversation, and I needed to keep my stupid mouth sh- "All gray."

Crap.

I said something when I should have said nothing.

Damn it.

They were the first words I'd uttered since "hello, nice to meet you" and they were in disagreement with the mother of the woman I had every intention of marrying. Both of the ladies turned to me. The elder of the two was the first to respond. "What was that, Steven?"

My wife's lips curled and she exposed her teeth. I think she might have growled. She wanted me to just shut up. She could see the light of the train steaming down the tracks. She knew exactly where this was headed.

My mouth punched my brain in the cerebellum and told it to shut the hell up. "Um. I just think that life is too complex to be pigeonholed into being either black and white. It's all one giant shade of gray. I mean, you would have to have not paid any attention at all to anything around you, to think that black and white makes any sense whatsoever when it comes to humanity."

My wife's jaw was hanging open. She looked as if she'd just watched me rape the house cat with a wooden spoon from the kitchen. Her hands coiled into fists and she blurted, "Steven! You can't disagree with my mom!"

Actually, I can – and I did.

I probably shouldn't have - at least not on the very first time I met the woman – but I did.

My mother-in-law seemed more than a little surprised as well. "I don't necessarily believe that, Steven. That's a pretty negative way to look at the world."

At that point, I really should have shut up. If I couldn't shut up, I should have punched myself in the face or wedged one of my testicles between my knuckles and twisted until I gave myself a ghetto vasectomy. Hell, maybe I should have gone with the face, followed by the nuts and finished off the trifecta with a good ol' fashioned titty-twister.

I should have leapt through the glass window behind me.

I should have set the couch on fire.

I should have challenged Anderson Silva to a street fight.

I should have moved to Florida, married Casey Anthony, and let her become the mother of my firstborn.

I should have done anything at all, other than continue talking.

"Eh, I don't know. I just think that's a pretty silly way to look at it."

WHAM! WHAM! WHAM!

That was Anderson Silva turning my face into pulsating, uncooked hamburger.

SIZZLE. SIZZLE. SIZZLE.

That was the crackle of my fiery couch.

TSK. TSK. TSK.

That was the sound of overly sensitive people vocalizing their disappointment in my Casey Anthony joke.

FLOATY PENS AND JEFF GORDON

FLOATY PENS AND JEFF GORDON

I've had many jobs in my life. Some of them I've liked. Most of them I've hated.

I started early. When I was fifteen-years-old, I began working as a checker at the local Kmart. I've also worked as a ride operator at Six Flags, and as a security guard at the very same place a couple of years later. In college, I worked as a driver helper for Pepsi, and I even spent a very small amount of time working in a meat packing plant on the Wisconsin border. In my adult years, I have been working on mostly art-related jobs.

There was a brief period of time when I was forced to clean the bathrooms of the local Best Buy and pick through bloody maxi-pads to make ends meet, but that's another story for another time.

This particular tale is about my very first art-related job.

How do you think it went?

Would I even be writing this, if it was all roses and candy, and summer treks through fields of dandelions?

Of course not.

I'd just moved to California to live with my wife. I was fresh out of college and I was anxious to tear into my exciting new life in the state of movie stars and expensive cars. Unfortunately, there weren't many expensive cars and there were even less movie stars where I was living.

There were a lot of very cheap cars, though. No movie stars either.

I think I saw a Dodge Stratus, once.

My tiny, backwoods new place of residence was called, Beaumont. It wasn't much to write home about – sort of like the town I'd grown up in, but very unlike the city I'd been living in. Most of the people had all of their teeth.

Well, three-fourths of them, anyway.

There was a general store, and the sheriff wore a cowboy hat and boots with spurs on the back, and every week there would be an old fashioned *hangin'* in the town square.

Okay, that was a lie.

Beaumont did have a local, southern-fried newspaper though, and that newspaper was called The Record Recorder. The stories featured within the pages of the Recorder were a hodgepodge of local weirdness. In fact, here's a headline pulled directly from the front page: "Snail Races Set at the Cherry Festival!"

Yep, Snail Races – with an exclamation point.

I basically lived in Mayberry.

I was hired at the Recorder as a Graphic Designer. It was my job to put together the various ads scattered between those incredible snail race stories. I pieced together advertisements for everything from local Realtors (who always insisted on including pictures of them that were no less than then twenty-years-old) to local restaurants, to the crazy lady that would sell knitted doggie clothes out of her garage.

How that crazy broad afforded an ad, I'm not entirely sure, but she did.

The sales people at the Recorder hated me because of my constant typos. The other two graphic designers were sort of indifferent to me because I never talked. The lady who answered the phone in the front office, and was obsessed with "*NASCAR driving sensation Jeff Gordon,*" disliked me immensely because I once asked her *nicely* to *please* not have everyone sing to me when my birthday rolled around.

She, of course, ignored my request and did it anyway.

Jerk.

Not only that, but she had them do it beside the life size Jeff Gordon cardboard cutout she kept next to her desk.

I wasn't even sure who Jeff Gordon was, but I suddenly hated the guy.

I think that everyone at the Recorder wished they were somewhere else.

The news people writing up *hard hitting* exposes on art shows at the local sixty-five and over gated community were bored. The poor bastards running a fifty-seven-year-old printing press in conditions that undoubtedly left them sterile were a smidge annoyed. The publisher with a four-year degree in communications, who never quite imagined he would spend his life putting out a paper firmly entrenched in minutia of snail racing, was more than a little disappointed in the way things had played out.

It was only a matter of time before one of them decided to show the world just how much they despised their situation.

Tuesday, 1:37PM

"What the hell?"

It was Jeff Gordon's number one fan. She was screaming at the top of her lungs and it was echoing throughout the tiny building.

Everyone could hear her. The other two graphic designers immediately leapt from their seats and jogged into the other room to see what was going on. I continued working.

Was it because I just didn't care or was it because I was too lazy? In truth, it was a little from column A, and a smidgen from column B.

Honestly, Jeff Gordon's number one fan could have been on fire and I might not have batted an eye.

What? What is it would you expect me to do? Put her out? No thanks. Fire burns and burning hurts. *I'm way too smart a feller' for that.*

My fellow designers returned to their desks ten minutes later. After an extended period of silence, I figured I should ask, so I did. "What happened?"

"Apparently, someone urinated in Janet's pen cup."

Gag.

Yep, you read that correctly. That wasn't a typo and the word *"urinated"* doesn't actually mean, *"putting fresh flowers into"* in the tiny town of Beaumont.

In the middle of the day, in a small but crowded office, and in plain view of just about anyone that might be strolling by, someone had the balls to fill a cup full of pens on Janet's desk with their piss.

When Janet returned to her desk after lunch, she found her pens bobbing up and down in a cup full of foamy, yellow, pungent goodness.

This was the Record Recorder, this was how much people hated working there, and this was how much they disliked their co-workers.

A few of weeks later, someone smeared poop all over the wall of the women's bathroom.

Once again, this incredible feat of ninja crapping was pulled off in the middle of the day.

I'm still not sure what hidden part of a person's brain suddenly fires and tells their body that it would be a good idea to grab a handful of freshly crapped feces and smear it on the walls.

How do they go right back to work after that?

For sanity's sake, I have to assume that both incidents were planned out months in advance. There were probably diagrams drawn, and scenarios worked out to the finest detail. They had to have been, because no one was ever caught.

Mr. or Mrs. PoopyHands McPissJar got away with it.

Wait. Maybe there were two of them - the Bonnie and Clyde of revolting, bodily function, workplace *"pranks."*

Needless to say, I wasn't all that heartbroken when I decided to quit the company and move onto the next chapter in my life.

It was really only a matter of time before someone decided to piss and/or shit on something that belonged to me.

Hell, if I'd had stayed there any longer, I might have joined in the fun myself.

THE SQUISHY WHITE BLISS

THE SQUISHY WHITE BLISS

My wife was lying beside me on the bed. We were watching television and enjoying each other's company, and having a rather pleasant night, when she leaned over, and, with one hand, turned my face in her direction.

I, of course, assumed she was looking for a smooch.

Unfortunately, when I puckered my lips and leaned into her, she shoved my head backward. Her eyes were trained on my forehead. Her expression was focused and determined, and she had no interest whatsoever in the pathetic smooch I'd offered up.

She was on a hunt.

Her eyes moved from my forehead, across my cheeks and over my nose. They were darting back and forth at an incredible rate. She wasn't finding what she was looking for. She bit her lower lip and moaned with a hint of frustration.

Annoyed, I felt the need to speak up. "What the hell are you doing?"

"Just looking."

"Looking for what?"

"Oh...nothing."

That was a lie. I knew it was a lie.

"You're obviously looking for something, hun."

"No…nothing. Really, I'm not looking fo-" Before she could finish her sentence her eyes lit up. She spotted something on my forehead and bared her teeth like Roy's tiger before it turned his face into a lunch buffet. She had spotted something on my forehead and her fingers reached for it with cobra-like speed.

I tried to shove her away, but, suddenly, she was stupid-strong. The adrenaline had kicked in and she had the strength of twelve women. "What the hell are you doing?"

She didn't respond.

Her fingers mashed together and a flash of pain shot across my forehead and down my face. It was a zit. She'd found a zit on my forehead and her energized fingers were attacking it from the sides. They had it surrounded. It was trapped, a hot, tight-booty piece of *"fresh meat"* who accidently dropped the soap in the prison shower, and much like the prisoners surrounding that poor unsuspecting sap, my wife's fingers had something similar on their mind – they wanted to *pop that sheeeet*.

The situation I've just described actually took place quite some years ago – not long after I'd moved in with my wife and not too long before we tied the knot. It was the first time anyone, including myself, had ever popped a zit on my face. In fact, up until that very instant, the idea of popping zits had never even entered my mind.

Call me crazy, or insane, or whatever you want to call me, but the thought of squeezing a red sore in order to see pus come shooting out wasn't exactly high on my bucket list.

A night of meaningless sex with Salma Hayek was pretty high, though.

It was number two, actually.

Eating the world's largest pizza was number one.

So I guess that sort of says a lot about me.

Despite the zit-popping revelation, I still married my wife. The positives outweighed the creepy zit weirdo negatives and I decided to roll the dice. In the years since we made it official, my wife's obsession with my face zits has only gotten worse.

I'm not even what most would consider a "zitty" guy, but if one popped up, she would immediately rub it out of existence.

It was genocide.

It was mass murder on levels that would have made even Idi Amin jealous.

It didn't matter where we were, or what we were doing. If she spotted a zit on my face, she had to destroy it. She was a madwoman. She'd gone bonkers. She was smiting zits like Zeus from the heavens above. She was blasting them like the Death Star taking out Alderaan.

At some point along the way, a very strange thing happened. Maybe it was all the blood and death, and the copious amounts of puss that had squirted from my pores, but I found myself warming to the idea.

There was something about the way my wife looked while popping, and chuckling, and grinning through tightly drawn lips. She seemed to be in ecstasy – ecstasy mixed with revulsion, but ecstasy, nonetheless.

You know, sort of like having an orgasm while sprawled atop a bed of cow plop.

Whatever it was, years after my first disgusting run-in with my zit-hunter bride, things had changed. I wanted to see what all the fuss was about. I wanted in.

The hunted was about to become the hunter.

Lets zoom ahead five years. Once again, the wife and I were lying in bed, and, once again, we were watching television. (Because we're basically a couple of lazy slugs.) Out of the corner of my eye, I spotted something red on the side of her face. It was right on her temple and, I swear to you, it seemed to be throbbing.

The throbbing was calling me.

It wanted me.

The little red blotch had a crystal white eyeball on the tip. Like a morphine addict, it was staring right at me, peering into the deepest, darkest parts my soul. It brought a shovel with it and it was digging even deeper than that. It was searching for the animistic, survival of the fittest, disgusting, plain old mean parts that are better left buried. It was looking for the parts that laugh when a guy gets hit in the groin with a flying object, or someone slips and falls on their ass, or when a serial killer kidnaps a young boy, rapes him, murders him, then rapes his corpse one more time for good measure.

Um, wait.

You know what?

Forget I typed that last bit.

I lunged at the bulging lump of disgust on my wife's face quicker than a hiccup, and with far worse intentions.

"Steven, what the hell are you doing?" She tried to push me away, but it was my turn to have the adrenaline and she didn't have a chance.

Plus, her lack of penis makes her naturally weak. That too.

(Send your letters of complaint to steven@stevensucks.org.jerk.shutup.)

I shoved her back to the bed. "I just have to get this one thing on your face!"

My fingers wormed themselves onto either side of the tiny, deformed, pus-filled nipple. Once they were in place, my nails dug in and began to squeeze!

Like a soft serve ice cream machine created by Beelzebub himself, the puss ripped through her flesh and began to spurt.

My wife screamed in pain. I barely heard her, and I honestly didn't care. My ears had gone deaf. My peepers were locked onto leaking blood and the ever-growing strand of puss already beginning to curl like a little albino pigtail.

I was there, in that bed, but I was somewhere else.

I was adrift in a disgusting, perverted, foul world of pure, squishy white bliss. Euphoria began to wash over me – the sort of euphoria that can only come from a string of puss resting gently on your fingernail like a disease-filled baby in its baby crib.

I'd seen God.

And God was zit puss.

When it was over, I held my disgusting treasure out for my wife to see. "Wow. Look at that. Holy crap, you're disgusting."

She rubbed her head and shoved me away. "Ouch! What made you do that?"

"You've been doing it to me for years."

"So? That's different."

I looked at my wife. I looked at the puss.

The little light bulb above my head illuminated. Suddenly, everything seemed so clear. It was as if all the mysteries of the universe had folded into my pores and ticked my gray matter. Suddenly, I had a purpose. Suddenly, I had a reason for existing, and breathing. Suddenly, I understood everything, and suddenly, I knew what I had to do.

I told her to eat it.

She slugged me in the chest.

Goats Eat Cans Volume 3

NEVER PICK STANGE OBJECTS OFF THE FLOOR

NEVER PICK STRANGE OBJECTS OFF THE FLOOR

The wife and I have a cat. That cat's name is Tom.

Yeah, I know, real original, right?

Listen, I didn't name the annoying little bastard, so lay off.

Tom has been a part of my wife's life for years. He was round long before I came into the picture. He's a thousand-years-old. He's Mummra, the Ever Living. He's gray, and he's going bald around his ears, and he's built like a plumped up Christmas goose with a second Christmas goose in its belly. He's huge.

In this particular instance, when I say "*huge,*" I actually mean "*fucking enormous!*" A few years back, we managed to wrangle the pudgy son of a bitch onto a digital scale and it let us know that he weighed nearly twenty-two pounds.

That's pretty damn big.

Garfield wasn't that big, and he ate nothing but Lasagna and, occasionally, Dr. Liz Wilson's crotch.

What?

You don't remember that happening? Garfield orally satisfying John's love interest, you don't think that ever happened? You don't recall ever reading that strip? Believe it or not, Jim Davis was a heavy drinker. It's in his "*personal collection.*" I was lucky enough to get a look at it during a comic book convention in the spring, 1992.

No more comments from the peanut gallery. *Let me finish my story.*

Though Tom began his life as an outdoor cat, he's spending his twilight years inside. When we first met, Tom would grace us with his presence long enough for us to feed him and send him on his way. He was like a chubby Rambo. He was living in the woods and digging in the dirt, and feasting on the blood of his kills and the mashed up goop we'd leave for him in a dish near the backdoor.

One morning, after waking up, taking my morning shower, scrubbing my junk and soaping the crack of my backside, I sauntered into the bedroom with nothing more than a towel around my waist.

Oh, yeah. Sounds pretty sexy, huh?

Actually, no.

It's really kind of gross. Don't try to picture it. Really, just don't. The image will get stuck in your brain. It'll brand itself to your gray matter and that's exactly where it'll stay. It'll fold into the crevasses of your brain like my hand into the crack of my soapy rear. You'll regret it, if you do. My body isn't so great. It's kind of like a six-foot tower of water balloons filled with pudding and glued together with lumpy cake frosting.

I was running a bit late that morning, and only had ten minutes to get dressed, get my ass out the door, and get to work. While I wasn't exactly in *love* with my job at the time, showing up late simply wasn't an option. I had bills to pay and mouths to feed, and fat cats to get fatter, and soap to buy in order to scrub my ass.

Why do I keep bringing that up?

You don't want to hear about my ass. I don't even want to hear about my ass. My ass often tries to pretend it's not an ass at all.

It wants to be a director – a lady director – of various fresh-scented lady films.

I don't know what that means.

I was on my way to the closet to find garments to disguise my shameful nakedness when I spotted something on the floor.

What the hell?

It was lying next to the bed. It was tiny. It was something tiny and it was something gray, and there was just a hint of something brown speckled about it.

Was it poop?

Cat poop?

No, it didn't look like cat poop – not exactly the right texture. The color was off, too.

I scratched my head, tilted it to the side and moved just a bit closer.

What the diggity?

That's right, I said the word *"diggity"* in my head. And no, I'm not a peckerwood Will Smith, circa 1991.

The closer I moved, the more the details became clear. For a moment I thought it was a ball of twine - *slimy ball of twine, maybe?* A ball of twine that had recently been wedged between the slick beef flaps of my well-soaped booty?

I moved closer.

What the shiz?

With one hand, I reached forward and scooped the confusing slimy, gray, brownish-freckled lumpy sphere into my hand. I bobbled it around a few times and tested its weight. It wasn't heavy. It was too heavy to be twine and not heavy enough to be a stone, or even poop.

What the dongkers?

As I began rolling it back and forth in my palm, it flipped onto its backside and I suddenly realized exactly what I was holding.

It was a damn mouse head.

There wasn't a body attached, or even a neck. It was just a head. It was a severed mouse head with eyes so wide they looked like the candy peppers on a chocolate Easter bunny.

Its little mouth was opened wide and its tongue had the texture of an overcooked strip of bacon. Its tiny white teeth caught the light of the morning sun and reflected into my eyes.

That damn cat.

That stupid, chubby, bald headed, cat.

I was holding a decapitated mouse head.

The towel around my waist came loose and fell to the floor.

Suddenly, I was holding a decapitated head in the nude.

Jeffery Dahmer was the last person to do that.

My fat old cat was a dead man.

-Steven Novak-

THERE ARE GHOSTS IN MY HOUSE

THERE ARE GHOSTS IN MY HOUSE

My wife is scared of ghosts.

What's that, you say? "Ghosts aren't real and it sure is silly to be scared of ghosts."

Well, of course, it is. I know that ghosts aren't real, and you know that ghosts aren't real, and the dude who was in a coma for twenty years before *waking* up with a brain made up mostly of pudding mush and stool juice even knows that ghosts aren't real.

Sure, he can't tell up from down, left from right, or a penis from a vagina, but even he knows that the concept of ghosts is as silly as the "Spock's Brain" episode of the original Star Trek series.

My wife, however, still isn't so sure.

Like almost every other woman I've encountered over the course of my life, my beautiful and mostly sane wife can watch hour upon hour of gory forensic-related television, or become engrossed in all the grizzly details of the Tot-Mom murdering her kid trial, or O.J. chopping his wife's head off, or read books on actual murders – that actually happened - to actual, previously alive, human beings.

The woman is fascinated by woman drama, and suicides, and deaths. She's looked at pictures of crime scenes, and grieving families, and the dead-eyed stare of Nancy Grace's zombie-skinned 3/4 profile.

She loves all that stuff and absolutely none of it seems to affect her in any way, whatsoever.

And yet, I'm not allowed to watch Poltergeist.

How in the hell does that make sense?

This woman scoured the Internet just to catch a blurry glimpse of Kurt Kobain's real life brains.

Poltergeist, with its craptacular 80's special effects, downright laughable performance by Coach's Crag T. Nelson, and cartoony Disney spook animation is off limits, though?

She's a crazy person. She's a wackadoo.

To be perfectly honest, it makes me a little bit angry. I should be allowed to watch Poltergeist. I should. It shouldn't be off limits and I shouldn't get scolded when it's on. That's not right – *not when the trials of baby killers are allowed to hold our television hostage for three months at a time.*

Unfortunately, for my wife, when I get angry, I like to get revenge.

It was 4:30AM. It was October. I woke up, shuffled to the bathroom to expel my morning urine, and returned to the bedroom fully intending on sliding back into sleep – until I spotted my wife.

While I was away, she had managed to twist her body so that she was lying diagonally across the bed. She was stretched out. Her arms and legs were kicked wide as if she were making a snow angel. My spot was gone. There was no bed left.

Jerk.

I gave her a shove. "Hey, scooch over."

She didn't move.

I wedged my hands into her side and tried rolling her over.

She smacked them away.

I pressed my elbow into her spine and tried again.

She kicked me in the face.

Jerk!

I was tired, I was feeling frustrated, and I was annoyed. I was moments from placing a pillow over her head and pressing until her arms stopped flailing, when it hit me.

It was like an ACME brand anvil had been dropped on my head in a Bugs Bunny short. It was like I'd been the recipient of a swift kick to the wobbeldy-woos by an NFL place kicker. It smacked me like a North Korean nuclear bomb test in my brain. I was through fighting her physically. Alternate tactics were required.

I left the bedroom, headed downstairs and into the kitchen.

Won't let me watch scary movies, huh?

Take up my side of the bed, huh?

For every action there is an equal, and opposite, reaction, jerkface.

One-by-one, I began opening the kitchen cabinets. I opened them and I left them opened. The high ones, the low ones; I opened them all and left them wide.

It was a little idea I'd picked up from a scene in the Sixth Sense *(which I had to sneak around to watch)*, a couple years prior. It was subtle and it was weird, but I had exhausted traditional tactics and I needed something subtle and weird.

I knew that when she came downstairs and spotted the opened cabinets she wasn't going to know what to make of it. It wasn't blatantly scary, but it was certainly unsettling - *which really is the perfect kind of scary, anyway.*

She was going to plotz.

When I finished, I returned upstairs and curled my body into a fetal position on an open area near the bottom of the bed. Half my body was hanging off the edge and I didn't have a pillow, or a blanket, or a covering of any kind. I knew that when I woke up, I was going to be sore. My spine was going to be twisted and the cartilage rubbed raw. My legs were going to hurt and my arms would be sore and I was going to spend the next few hours shivering.

Yet, strangely enough, I had a smile on my face.

It was going to be worth it.

When I woke up and managed to uncoil my crumpled limbs, my wife had already showered. She was clean, and she was dressed and she was about to leave for work. She said goodbye to me, gave me a peck on the lips, and headed downstairs. The moment she entered the kitchen, everything went silent.

It stayed that way for nearly five minutes.

Then I heard this, "Steven!"

She was screaming at me. Her voice cracked when she reached the *"n"* in my name. I forced my creaky bones to carry me into the hallway. I leaned over the banister just as she bounded into the family room and looked up at me with a pair of wide, terrified eyes. She was breathing heavy. Her hands were coiled into fists.

I tried not to laugh. "What is it?"

"Shut up, Steven. You know exactly what it is."

I swallowed my chuckles and tightened my anus to keep them from farting out the backside. I played it stupid. I played it half asleep. "Huh?"

"Shut up."

"Shut up what? What are you talking about?"

"Stop it!"

"Stop what? What the hell are you talking about?"

She paused for a moment before saying it, as if she expected a ghost to appear from nowhere, wrap his arms around her and carry her screaming to hell. "The cabinets."

There was a confused look on her face that I found both priceless and hilarious. I swallowed back my laughter like a load of gooey-man syrup and wasn't the least bit ashamed. *In fact, it tasted pretty damned delicious.*

"Yeah, what? What about them?"

It was working. My acting was spot on and it was working perfectly. My wife was buying it. That ghost-believing goofball was really buying it! In her brain, these open cabinets were the work of ghosts. It was as simple as that. Of course, they were. What else could they have been?

"The cabinets, Steven...in the kitchen. The cabinets are open..."

"Maybe it was the cat, you know how he does that sometimes."

She looked back at the kitchen, then back at me, then back at the kitchen. Her brain was trying to figure out if the cat was an actual option. The cat made sense for the cabinets on the floor, but not the ones up high.

No, the cat didn't make sense.

She stepped further away from the kitchen. I think a very real part of her thought Slimer would come charging out of it and slam his blobby green body into her chest.

Personally, I'd be more afraid of Dan Akroyd doing the same, but maybe that's just me.

"No. All of them are opened. Even the ones up high!"

I shrugged my shoulders. "I don't know what to tell you."

"Shut up! You did it! This isn't funny, Steven. Not at all!"

"Look, I didn't do anything. When would I have done it? I've been asleep. I don't know what to tell you. "I think I grinned just a little bit when the next words seeped from between my lips. "Maybe it was ghosts or something."

Game. Set. Match.

I left the railing, headed back into the bedroom and spread out across the bed. I didn't have to be up for another hour, and *damn it*, I was going to enjoy it.

"Steven!"

I told myself that the next time she stole the covers from me and made me sleep like a leather-clad gimp in a sex-box at the foot of the bed, the cabinet ghost was going to put on a repeat performance.

Hell, maybe he'd even open up all of her tampons, cover them in blood that looked suspiciously like ketchup, and spread them across the bathroom floor.

He's a wily one, that cabinet ghost.

I THINK SHE'S BEAUTIFUL. WHAM!

I THINK SHE'S BEAUTIFUL. WHAM!

My wife has a very weird habit. If I say something nice to her, and it makes her even the slightest bit embarrassed, she punches me.

They aren't playful punches either. Nope, this broad puts her hips into it. She swings with everything she has. She generally wallops me with a full-on, full force, closed fist worthy of Ivan Drago himself, sort of punch.

And most of the time she smashes me right in the spine.

The bones in my back are pretty much loose bits of gravel, at this point.

A few years ago, some of my wife's family came to visit and she decided that it might be fun to take everyone on a trip to the San Diego Zoo. The drive would be something close to three hours and the cars would be packed, and the associated costs would be more than we could afford, but what the hell, right? I'd never been there. And animals are interesting enough, I guess.

There was a possibility that the monkeys might throw some poop.

So that was worth a car ride with all my *nutty* in-laws.

I guess.

Maybe.

Eh, it's too close to call.

Maybe if they were trained animals? You know, if they were doing back flips, or handstands, or writing Justin Bieber lyrics and Twilight books, and burrowing their way into the flesh of the Real Housewives of WereAllTerribleHumanBeingsandSomeoneShouldPunchusinourVaginas? Maybe then it would have been worth it?

Maybe not.

Surprisingly, the three-hour drive went smoother than I ever imagined it could and we arrived at the zoo fresh faced and optimistic. We spent the morning walking around, looking at the various animals, and inhaling that oh, so aromatic, *zoo smell* into our noses.

You know the smell I'm talking about. It's an odd mixture of a hot dog stand, rancid guacamole dip, and, of course, elephant plop.

My wife, her mother, and myself ended up in front of the lion cages. The rest of the rowdy clan was a little further down, gawking at the tigers and the bears.

Oh, my.

Okay, maybe they weren't actually looking at tigers and bears. Maybe I just said they were so I could work in that stupid lions and tigers and bears joke that I'm guessing fell flat.

It was lame. I know it. I just had to. I know it's corny and I know it's as old as shit, but I just had to. If you don't like it, bite me. That's right, I said bite me, sucka. Bite me, chew on me and spit me out when I don't agree with your particularly discerning palette. What's done is done, titface.

I ain't taking it back, titface.

My mother-in-law was staring at my wife in that weird sort of way mothers sometimes stare at their kids. It was loving, but it was also a bit creepy. If a stranger were to stare at you the same way, you'd call the cops. It's normal when a mother does it, though.

You lived in her vagina.

My wife noticed the look and it was clearly making her uncomfortable. She was shuffling in place and sighing. She dug her hands into her pockets and shrugged her shoulders. "What? What are you looking at?"

Her mother immediately looked away from her and toward me. "Steven, isn't my daughter beautiful?"

I was actually thinking to myself that she looked kind of sweaty and gross as a result of walking around in the one hundred and three degree weather for the last four hours. I couldn't very well go and blurt that out though, could I?

Instead, I choose the response I thought would allow me to keep my genitals intact. "Yep. She sure does, at that."

Immediately after the words left my mouth, it dawned on me that they were actually sort of true. Even as sweaty as she was and as gross as she looked, with her hair a complete mess and her make-up running down her perspiring cheeks, she was still a pretty beautiful looking woman.

I'd chosen my lady well.

My wife was embarrassed by the whole conversation. She didn't want people talking about her and she certainly didn't want them gushing over her. Her face was turning red. It was a cute sort of red-pink, really. The dimples in her chipmunk cheeks sprang to life and her head lowered as she tried to fight back a smile.

I chuckled.

In that moment, I realized just how very lucky a man I really was. I was lucky to find her, and I was even luckier to convince her to be my wife. Her nervousness was cute. She was cute. She accepted me for who I was, and she had stood by me even when I might not have deserved being stood by. Suddenly I wanted to kiss her. I wanted to wrap her in my arms and tell her ju...

WHAM!

She punched me in the back with everything she had.

She punched me so hard that I could almost swear I could hear her hand break.

"AGH!" I screamed so loud that every animal in the zoo simultaneously leapt into the air, dropped a fear dump, and started running in circles. Little children dropped their ice cream cones and grabbed hold of their parent's legs. The glass in the penguin cage shattered and sent the poopy penguin water splashing onto everyone standing nearby.

Like a bolt of lightning, a shock of pain at the point of impact traveled along my fractured vertebrae and into my legs. My knees buckled and I lurched forward. A nearby railing was the only thing that kept me from smashing into the concrete and shattering my face.

When I managed to turn toward my attacker, I noticed that she was breathing heavily and her fists remained clenched. She was sporting a "crazy eyez killa" sort of look that bottomed out the pit already settling in my stomach. She looked like she wanted to punch me again. My hands went up and my chin went down.

It was a fight or flight situation and I was ready to go!

I tried to steady my legs. "What the hell!" I had to be ready for anything.

While I was suddenly fighting for my life, my mother-in-law was cracking up. While the bones in my back were snapping, crackling and popping like the infamous breakfast cereal, she was having a good ol' time.

When the bloodlust eventually cleared from my wife's eyes, I relaxed my posture, lowered my fists and began to massage the searing pain coursing along the nerves in my upper back.

The wife reached for me. "I'm sorry, Steven..."

I batted her hand away. "Sorry? You just made me a cripple. Sorry? Sorry isn't going to cut it. Why did you do that?"

"I just got embarrassed."

And thus it began.

These days, she doesn't even use the whole *"embarrassment"* thing as an excuse for punching me in the back. At some point along the way, the act transformed from something she *couldn't* control to something she really enjoyed doing. The woman loves punching me.

In the morning, when I get out of bed - WHAM!

When she gets home from work - BLAMMO!

During dinner - POWZA!

After sex – YOWZA!

She says it's my fault. She claims that if I didn't react so funny when she did it, she wouldn't want to do it.

So, pretty much, she's a jerk and she's insane.

When I'm fifty and confined to a wheelchair because of repeated blows to the lower lumbar area, and she has to change my crap-filled diapers because my limited movement makes it impossible for me to do it myself, she won't think it's so funny.

Hope you like the scent of a grown man's underpants load, my beautiful wife.

-Steven Novak-

MY IMAGINARY FRIEND

MY IMAGINARY FRIEND

I guess I'm sort of a liar.

Wait just one minute. Don't go taking that the wrong way. I'm a liar, but I'm not some nasty, evil lying jerk that lies for the wrong reasons and hurts everyone around him because of it.

I don't go around telling poor little sick kids that they're going to be fine because I just discovered that the cure for their ailment is to eat a Snickers bar wrapped in a pancake once a day while listening to old Debbie Gibson tracks and watching reruns of H.R. Puffnstuf.

I don't make a point to call my mother up on the weekends and say, "Mom, you're never going believe it, but my wife is pregnant," only to laugh in her face when she finds out it's not true and that the closest she's ever going to get to grandchildren from me are the ones that die in my chopped up vas deferens.

What I'm trying to say is that I'm not a mean liar. *I lie for the sake of comedy.*

Plus, I don't really lie to anyone other than my wife.

You see, my wife and I have this weird little game we like to play - and by "we", I actually mean "me."

She hates it.

She hates me for playing it.

Which only makes me want to play it more.

It's a simple game, really. Basically, I tell her outlandish, completely insane lies, she listens to me prattle on like an idiot, and I chuckle quietly at my own unfunny jokes.

Sounds awesome, right?

The whole thing started quite a few years ago.

"How was your day, Steven?"

"Eh, you know, same old stuff."

"Oh."

I wish I could have offered something a bit more interesting to her, but, basically, that was the gist of it. I hated my job at the time, I was bored day in and day out while I was there, and there wasn't a whole hell of a lot more to say about it.

Or was it?

"There was one thing, though..."

"Oh, yeah, what?"

"I had lunch with John Lithgow."

I don't know where it came from. Seriously, I have no idea. I mean, John Lithgow? Why did I choose to go with John Lithgow? Of all the people on the planet Earth, I settled on Lithgow?

I mean, he's done a few decent flicks, sure.

Why Lithgow?

The world is chock full of somewhat interesting human beings. Louis C.K. is a funny guy. Rosario Dawson is a good-looking gal Stephen Hawking is pretty damn smart. Stan Lee created half the Marvel universe. Rosario Dawson has an incredible chest. Mark

Oliver-Everett writes some fantastic music. Rosario Dawson's backside looks great in leather. There are people that have done things, and seen things, and accomplished things far beyond that of character actor John Lithgow.

John Lithgow is the racing stripe on the tighty whities of Hollywood.

His career used to be a little thicker and a whole lot more noticeable. The years, and repeated washings in Cold Water Tide with bleach have mostly washed him away.

I've kept up with my John Lithgow stories for years.

John and I went half'sies on a place in Orange County a couple years ago and we threw some crazy-weird parties there before the neighbors asked us to leave. We've shared some good times, 'ol Liftgy and I.

We've also shared some women – the aforementioned Rosario Dawson being one of them.

I went to visit him, a few years ago, at his place on the beach. John kept the liquor flowing and I kept the ladies rolling. The next day, he invited me to the set of Dexter. Michael C. Hall personally asked me to direct a few scenes and come on in a supporting role. Ultimately, I had to decline. He was a nice guy – almost too nice. I didn't want to steal his thunder.

I met John in Catalina about a year ago. We played some jazz at a club downtown and spent the wee hours teaching a few "fresh off the bus" beauties how Hollywood really works on his yacht.

The Gowman came down with an STD.

Dude was picking scabs off his scrotum for weeks.

So that was pretty funny.

The other night, my wife *(who was obviously bored)*, asked me how things were between John and myself and I was forced to tell her of our falling out.

For some reason *(I'm guessing the boredom)* she played along. "Oh? What happened?"

"Well, he just had to go and ask me what I thought about the movie *Cliffhanger*. I told him not to, but he just had to do it. He said that he wanted me to be completely honest. He said he'd didn't want me to hold anything back."

By this time, my wife had lost interest and probably regretted saying anything in the first place. I continued anyway. "What the hell did he expect me to say? That I loved it? That I thought it was the next *Citizen Kane* and his performance dug its way into the pit of my soul? Anyway, I told him what I thought of it and we haven't spoken since. I called a couple times, but he won't return them. He's being a hard ass about it. "

At this point, my wife was only vaguely aware I was even in the room. She'd moved onto the remote and the television, and her responses were on cruise control. "That's rough, Steven."

"Damn straight, it's rough. It's sad when two friends drift apart. I've known the guy for nigh on twenty years. He was at my college graduation."

"No he wasn't."

"Yes he was."

"No he wasn't. I was there."

"He was in disguise. Trying to keep a low profile, you know!"

She turned from the television and stared at me with a look of utter confusion on her face. When she sighed, she sighed so deeply that the mole people living in the center of the Earth could hear.

"Steven?"

"What?"

"Why are you, like you are?"

I wonder if Big LithyJo will send me a Christmas card this year.

Hell, I wonder if I'll send him one.

I wonder if his wang scabs ever cleared up.

-Steven Novak-

KARMA AND DRUNKEN LADY BOOBS

KARMA AND DRUNKEN LADY BOOBS

It started innocently enough. I was upstairs in my office working when the doorbell rang. I skipped happily down the stairs *(because that's the only way to skip)*, opened the door and was greeted by, what I assumed was a seventeen-year-old girl. Standing beside her was a fifty-year-old woman dressed exactly like a seventeen-year-old girl.

I have no doubt she assumed the clothes were making her look twenty years younger, but she was wrong.

They were just making her look stupid.

Listen, I'm all for dressing how you want to dress, and doing whatever the hell you want to do to make yourself happy. I get that. That's an awesome way to look at life and I can respect that. At the same time, don't be annoyed when those wacko things you like to do make the world at large shake its head.

A pair of low rider jeans doesn't do a hell of a whole lot when it comes to the wrinkly forty-year smoker's skin, or the dreaded old lady elbows.

Also, a boob job looks odd enough on a lady of twenty-three.

It looks like something from the island of Dr. Moreau on a lady of fifty-four.

Don't deny it.

The younger of the two reached out and handed me an envelope. "Hi! We're your new neighbors from next door!" She was way too happy. *I find happiness unsettling.*

"We're having a little house warming party on Saturday, and you're welcome to come by."

I took the paper. "Alright. Thanks." Then I shut the door on them.

I had absolutely no intention of going to that party - none at all. The Hitler'stache had a better chance of making a comeback. Parties, and people, and people at parties just aren't my *thing*.

These days, my *thing* usually consists of watching Star Trek on DVD while lying around in my underwear and shoveling the contents of a bag of Cheetos into my mindlessly chomping jaws.

Sometimes I skip the underwear part.

Don't get me wrong, I hoped the party went well for my age-confused new neighbors and I wished them all the best, and would consider sending over a fruit basket or some such nonsense, but honestly...blah, blah, blah, whatever.

Screw it.

I tossed the flyer in the trash and headed back upstairs.

By 7PM, the party across the street was jumping. It was loud as hell, and the base was booming, and the laughter was rattling my ears, but it was only 7PM. Such things are perfectly acceptable at 7PM.

By 9PM, it was still going strong. The music was still cranked, the street was overstuffed with cars and there were a few people passed out on the lawn. It was only 9PM, though - so, that's cool – I guess.

I'm not a complete Scrooge. Sure, I have a black heart, and sure, I can't stand parties. I know how the world works though. I'm not an idiot.

It isn't everyone that chooses the life of a hermit.

I needed to keep that in mind.

I had to accept that.

Unfortunately, by midnight, nothing had changed. Not a single solitary thing. Something should have changed. It was midnight. My annoyance level was rising and the fact that the song "My Humps" was blasting so loudly that it was shaking the very foundations of my house wasn't helping matters any.

"My humps, my humps, my lovely lady lumps!"

AGH!

Pop music has a long history of moronic, moneymaking hits because the vast majority of people are morons. I get it. It's the way things are and it won't be changing anytime soon. *I really hate that song, though.*

It makes me feel like someone unscrewed my head, pulled out my brain, dropped a slow-slither Cleveland steamer into the cavity, then screwed the top back on and offered me a Pixie Stick.

Duger dastes dood!

I tried to remind myself to stop acting like such an old man. I needed to get over it. Normal people like to party. Normal people like to get hammered. Normal people like to pass out on the lawn. Normal people like to throw up in public toilets and on the side of the road. Normal people like the company of other normal people.

Normal people are morons, but they are who they are and there was absolutely nothing I could do about. I needed to accept the normal people and try to get some sleep.

I needed to ignore the screaming, and the yelling, and the lovely lady humps and let the simple-brains have their fun.

And that's exactly what I tried to do.

By 2AM, the shit was still going on.

There were cars peeling out of the cul-de-sac. "My Humps" had been replaced with something I wasn't really familiar with, but was equally asstacular in a homosexual, German-techno sort of way.

Apparently, someone in the neighborhood had decided to call the cops because a bunch of the drunken idiots charged into the middle of the street and began screaming defiant gibberish through the spaces in their vodka-stained teeth.

There is a fine line between being a rebel and being a complete asshole, and these morons were taking a piss on it.

3AM rolled around and still the same ol' shit.

Apparently the cops had better things to do.

3:30AM and more of the same.

I wasn't able to sleep for more than five minutes at a time. My legs were jittery and my hands clenched into fists. I wanted to kill the Black Eyed Peas. I wanted to murder Jim Beam. I wanted to kill and murder my wife for having the smarts to pop a sleeping pill earlier in the evening.

During one of my wife-minute naps, I was awoken by the sound of someone screaming outside. "Get the fuck outta my house! Get the fuck outta my fucking house you fucking fucker!"

What the hell? *Fucking fucker?* Who said fucking fucker? Why would someone say fucking fucker?

It was a woman's voice - some potty mouth gal who apparently had an issue with some fucking fucker.

I stumbled over to the window, peeked through the blinds and immediately noticed that it was the older woman from the previous day. She looked haggard as all hell. She looked like a drunk who got locked in the Budweiser plant over night and just went nuts. She looked like someone who'd been skinny dipping in the brewing tanks. There were hops in her hair and barley in her cooch.

My drunken grandma of a neighbor was sticking halfway out of a tan, open car door as it started to pull away. She was jogging alongside it, while at the same time trying to keep her shirt from falling off her left shoulder and exposing her silicone-stuffed milk maker to the early morning air.

She was failing.

Maybe it was wrong of me, but I smiled.

I smiled big.

It was a wide smile and it was a satisfied smile, and it was a smile so smileriffic that it almost looked like it was created in post-production.

Maybe that makes me a bad person.

I dunno.

I guess I also don't care.

This boob-exposed idiot kept me up all night with her nonsense. And why? Because she was trying a little bit too hard to be friends with her daughter, instead of her mother, or even an adult, or slightly less of an idiot.

I wasn't the slightest bit sorry that her night hadn't turned out exactly the way she'd hoped.

Unless her goal from the beginning was to end up looking like a booze- soaked mummy, with comic book boobs, inches away from getting run over by a red Firebird driven by a chubby bald guy, with a gold cross dangling in the forest of his gray chest hair, who seems to think it's still 1985.

If that was what she was shooting for, I suppose congratulations are in order.

PACEY JOE ON THE RADIO

PACEY JOE ON THE RADIO

Let me preface this little story by stating something that I've stated a million times before: I'm a big ass mess when it comes to social situations.

When I say the word mess, I don't mean that I'm mess on the level of a poopy baby diaper.

Oh, no.

I'm a much bigger mess than that. *Baby poop don't have shit on me.*

Imagine a very large, very hairy, grown man. Now wrap the oiled up rolls of his beef ham posterior into a filthy beach towel the same way you might wrap a baby in a diaper. Before you do that, spend the day feeding him a steady diet of Mexican food and leftovers from the Long John Silver's down the street.

Now, let that festering belly of nastiness squish up some poop, squeeze it through his rectum, and spread it across his cheeks.

Take that image, double it, and we're getting a little bit closer to my ultimate mess level.

Some years ago, I was asked by a friend if I had any interest in making an appearance on her Internet Radio Talk Show (which no longer exists) to talk about the very first edition of "Goats Eat Cans." I knew it was a bad idea, and I knew I shouldn't do it.

It was going to end badly. It just had to end badly.

Still, despite knowing that nothing good could come from it, I agreed.

Not only did I agree, but I wasn't even that nervous about it, which is weird.

Too weird, really.

The show was scheduled for a Sunday night and I was supposed to call in at 8:30PM.

At 6:00PM, I was still feeling pretty good about the whole thing. I wasn't the least bit nervous. I wasn't worrying about what I would say, or how I would say it, or sweating over whether or not I'd be funny. In fact, I wasn't worried about anything. Instead, I was sitting in the bedroom flipping through the channels without a care in the world.

There was an episode of "The Simpsons on." *I love The Simpsons.*

"So, are you getting nervous about tonight?"

That was my wife.

"No. Not really."

That was me.

"Wow. I' surprised you're not worried. Usually you'd be worried by now. You know, about it going really bad, or being boring or stuff. Good for you for not being worried."

That was my wife ruining my evening.

Damn it. Damn it. Damn it. Shit. Damn it. Shit. Ass Damn.

She couldn't just keep her mouth shut for a couple more hours? Really? All she had to do was zip her lips for two measly hours, but no. She couldn't. Instead, she went and mashed some doubt into my wackadoo brain.

She knew how my brain worked! She knew, damn well, what a mess it was up there!

In my brain, birds are called horses and horses are called pigs! Pigs don't even have a name! Pigs are made of Logos and coated in goat's blood! Blood consists mostly of high fructose corn syrup and the sweat of Cab Calloway!

In my brain, people reading this actually recognize the name Cab Calloway and consider it a viable pop culture reference!

What was my wife thinking?

8:00PM rolled around and I couldn't get her stupid warnings out of my head. By 8:15PM, my head was coated in sweat and my penis had shriveled away. By the time the clock struck 8:25PM, I was ready to jump out of my skin.

At 8:30PM, on the nose, I shuffled downstairs to make the call.

I could barely breathe. My sweaty-fat fingers struggled to dial the numbers. I couldn't imagine myself being able to formulate words, or answer questions. The very idea seemed insane.

When she asked me the first question, I opened my mouth and nothing emerged. My voice box was gone. It had been stolen. Mayor McCheese captured and prosecuted the Hamburgler one too many times. He'd given up on burgers and moved onto human organs.

I think I burped.

Something in my throat gurgled, anyway.

I eventually find my voice, then I spent the next hour pacing back and forth in my living room, trying to answer questions with something other than an incoherent grunt, all while trying to be just a little bit funny.

My jokes sucked, and I was failing – badly.

I was failing worse than Michael Jordan failed at baseball. I was failing worse than Madonna failed at acting. I was failing worse than the guy who played Kenickie in Grease failed at life after Grease.

I fumbled over my words. A sentence that made perfect sense in my head traveled south and emerged from my mouth seeming more like Charles Manson's prison ramblings. I was spewing nonsense - the kind of nonsense that is usually reserved for brain-fried hobos on street corners, or the nightly news.

I said that I hated kids and had no interest in giving them candy on Halloween, while, in the same breath, I mentioned that I made a living doing illustrations for children's publications.

I said that I didn't consider myself a writer because I didn't hang out in coffee shops and talk about politics.

I managed to call anyone who reads my blog or buys my book a moron, and I didn't even mean it in a reverse psychology sort of way.

I claimed that walrus vagina was the best vagina of all vagina.

Okay, no I didn't.

That would have actually been funny.

As I babbled and rambled and begged for it to end, my friend kept saying to her producer, "Well, do we have any calls, yet?"

"Any calls, yet?"

"So, um. Do we have any calls, yet?"

The answer to her question was always "no."

She really should have stopped asking.

Feeling my pain from the other side of the house and wanting badly to save me, my wife decided to call into the show from upstairs.

Oh, Jeezus.

This was the equivalent of your mom picking you up from high school in her Dodge Stratus and proceeding to wipe the "smutch" from your face in front of all your buddies. It was the kind of thing that got you beat up after gym class.

The interview was supposed to get archived and put up on the website that conducted it. I was informed the next day that they had some sort of technical problems and it was lost forever

I was disappointed.

And Britney Spears is our nation's greatest talent.

THOSE ARE JUST ACTORS, DOOFUS

THOSE ARE JUST ACTORS, DOOFUS

What do you think most normal people go to Las Vegas for? Booze? Whores? Gambling? Sex? Gambling on possible STD's and pouring booze down the cleavage of whores? Maybe, to begin what will, undoubtedly, be a failed marriage?

I'll tell you what most *normal* people don't go to Las Vegas for: *Star Trek*.

Mr. Spock and the Vegas strip don't necessarily go together like peanut butter and jelly or Mel Gibson and hatred.

If you've ever read anything that I've written, you should know that I'm anything but *normal*. I'm weird, and I'm a nerd and I like nerdy things, and because of my extreme nerdiness, I've been to Las Vegas twice – specifically for *Star Trek*.

Are you fighting the urge to give me a wedgie? Admit it. You are.

Maybe you want to dunk my head in the toilet and flush? Grab hold of my nips and twist until you hear my flesh tear? Kick me in the scones, and then kick me again for using the word scones?

No problem at all. I get it. I completely understand. And, honestly, you aren't the first.

My head is quite dunkable.

It's fun watching my faux-hawk swirl.

Here's the deal; the Hilton in Las Vegas had a little something called "The Star Trek Experience" and it's pretty much nerd heaven.

Seriously, I'm not a religious man by any means, but if there is a God, I'm guessing that He resides somewhere between the row of Next Generation mugs and the Porthos stuffed toys in the gift shop.

This place gives me a boner that makes my Rosario Dawson boner look like a Drew Barrymore boner by comparison – *which is barely a boner, at all.*

It makes me feel like Augustus Gloop, the moment he first waddled into Wonka's chocolate factory and began to salivate.

I think I should mention that Agustus also had a boner in the original film.

Check the Special Edition Director's Cut, pause the moment before he topples into the chocolate and zoom in on his little shorts. You'll see it.

I want everything at *The Experience* to be mine. I want to take it home with me, and stack it on my desk and stare at it lovingly. I want to read it, and play with it, and pop it into my DVD player. I want to drop my pants and make sweet love to it.

My wife, of course, hates *The Experience* and she hates the dumb look on my face when I'm there.

"Why do we have to go on that stupid ride again?"

"Steven, you're not really going to spend seventy dollars to get your picture taken in that captain's chair again, are you?"

"Can't we leave, and go see a show or something? Maybe we can get tickets to Cirque Du Soleil?"

Cirque Du Soleil? Seriously? This woman had the nerve to suggest Cirque Du Soleil to me? Batshit crazy. Batshit-fucking-crazy.

She once had the gall to actually suggest Celine Dion as a viable substitute for all things Star Trek.

I almost hit her in the face with a brick and buried her in the desert beside Fat Jimmy Stampanato.

It's one thing to not "*get*" my weirdo obsession with all things Trek. Fine. I can understand that. Okay, maybe not understand it as much as accept it, but still.

It's another thing entirely to suggest Celine Dion as an alternative. That's nonsense. It's lunacy. It's fifty steps backward, right over a cliff and into a tank full of maneating Great Whites with lasers on their heads and chainsaws for teeth.

It's the sort of thing that gets a happily married woman served with a stack of divorce papers, if she's not careful.

At *The Experience,* they have a simulator ride called the "Borg Encounter." Before you actually get on the *ride,* your group is led through a series of decently constructed sets, while explosions go off around you and actors pretending to be Starfleet officers play out a scenario in which the Borg are attacking the space station you're supposed to be on.

It's petty sweet.

It's Agustus Gloop boner sweet.

Also, when the actors aren't looking, I like to touch all the fake buttons and pretend I'm firing photon torpedoes.

Shut up. It makes me smile.

At one point during the tour, our group of space tourists was *huddled* in a cargo bay as the ship *exploded* around us. Suddenly, the lights went out. My wife grabbed my arm and squeezed.

What the hell?

Was she scared?

The sound of an explosion blasted through the speakers in the wall behind us. A cloud of smoke came rushing into the room. My wife moved from my side and slid behind me. She buried her head in the crook of my armpit.

She *was* scared.

Holy Toledo, the doofus love of my live was honestly, no joke-scared!

She was also using me as a human shield from the fictional danger, but that's a whole other discussion.

A group of three guys dressed in Borg costumes slowly began to walk through the twisted metal and billowing clouds. They were moving in our direction and the little red laser beams on their eyes were flashing off our touristy garbs.

My wife was peeking through the crack between my armpit and my torso like a terrified five-year-old with urine running down her leg. She was breathing fast. Sweat was pouring down her face; her nails had punctured the flesh of my arm and were digging into the muscle underneath.

She'd clearly lost her mind. "What the hell are you doing?"

"What?"

"What are you doing? Are you scared?"

"N-no..."

The dudes dressed as the Borg - who likely worked part time at the Best Buy just outside of town - were barely ten feet away when the *"resistance is futile"* warning roared from a speaker system above our heads. At least, that's what I think happened. It sounded about as clear as the ordering window at a Burger King. My wife ducked her head out of sight and mashed her face into the center of my back.

I chuckled. I had to. She just looked so damn silly. "Shut up. You're really scared, aren't you?"

"No."

"You do know that those are just guys in costumes, right?"

"I know that."

"Then what's the problem?"

"Well…what if their circuitry goes haywire or something? You don't know."

Circuitry?

Wha?

Circuitry?

Screw it. I didn't have the energy to respond.

I may be a dork and a nerd, and I might be a loser of the absolute highest order, and my strange man-love for Captain Picard could be considered morally reprehensible in the eyes of the fundamentalist Christians out there, but at least I'm not my wife.

My wife thinks the fake Borg guys have *circuitry*.

NEED SOME CRACK? ASK MR. WHITE

NEED SOME CRACK? ASK MR. WHITE

To passersby, the little cul-de-sac I lived on a few years back looked rather quiet and unassuming. It wasn't Mayberry by any stretch of the imagination, but it was usually peaceful and plain, and quaint. It was decent little suburban hideaway to start a family in - maybe raise some cute, stinky-diapered kids and watch them grow into not so cute, stinky-assed adults.

Looks can be deceiving.

If you don't believe me, just ask the poor saps that ended up with their heads wrapped in plastic and stored in Jeffery Dahmer's freezer.

"Sure, I'll go back to your place weird little man with the big glasses. Sure, I'll smoke some weed with you and have a couple beers. Sure, I'll let you measure the circumference of my skull and compare it to the width of your Igloo cooler. What's the worst that can happen?"

Soon afterward, their arms were separated from their torsos, and Jeff was on the other end of the room with his pants down, humping away the bloody goo and muscle tissue of their shoulder hole.

I know that I've written about the party house across the street from me before - with their early morning parties and their half-naked adults who like to chase cars down the street. I might have also mentioned their soccer hooligan, drunk off their ass, morning brawls in the street and the constant appearances by the cops.

In the house to our left, there lived some punk ass twelve-year-olds who told me to "fuck off" while I retrieved the paper one morning.

In the house next to them, there was a forty-year-old father who acted more like a fifteen-year-old d-bag, and in the house next to them, there lived an old man that sat in his folding chair, wearing only a housecoat and a pair of slippers, and proceeded to stare at the street all day, every day.

As annoying as all of those wackos might have been, none of them ever came close to scaring me the way the guy who lived in the house on our right did.

In fact, they aren't even in the same ballpark.

One afternoon, I was on my way back from the mailbox at the end of the block. I was passing by my neighbor's driveway when three vans came speeding into the cul-de-sac and skidded to a stop directly in front of his house – which, at the moment, also happened to be directly in front of me.

What the hell?

I stopped dead in my tracks. My legs locked in place and my hand crushed the mail it was holding. My heart kicked into overdrive and my sphincter closed tight.

All at once, van doors opened and guys with mustaches and vests of the bullet halting variety piled out.

My mind turned to jelly. "Holy shit. Are they after me? What the hell did I do? Maybe it's a bizarre case of mistaken identity? Maybe I'm actually a government agent who was given a drug-induced case of amnesia and a fake life in order to keep the delicate government secrets locked inside my head from ever seeing the light of day? Am I Jason Bourne? Am I Arnold Schwarzenegger in

Total Recall? Maybe I'll have to fight them all off utilizing the superior training that has, until this moment, remained dormant! I'll have to steal one of their vans! I'll have to head to NASA. I can hijack a space shuttle there! I can take it to Mars and meet creepy belly-men and have a late night rendezvous with that lady with the three boobs! Maybe I'll have to ta…"

They ran right past me and swarmed my neighbor's door.

Sigh. I was sort of looking forward to motorboating three boobs.

The lead guy with the thickest vest and the bushiest mustache arrived first at my neighbor's door and pounded on it three times. "Mr. White! Open up, Mr. White! We know you're in there!"

I'm not even joking when I tell you that the guys name was Mr. White. This was long before *Breaking Bad* ever hit the air, and it made the show even cooler for me when it did.

Mr. White was inside. He said something, but I couldn't quite make it out. This was mostly because I had decided it would be in my best interest to beat some serious feet and put as much space in between me and the guys with the giant battering ram and the automatic firearms.

"Come on, Mr. White! Don't make this any harder than it has to be! Open up! We just need to talk to you! There won't be a problem, if you open up!"

I was only hearing one end of the conversation, but it sounded like Mr. White was stalling. Maybe he was pouring his drugs down the toilet, or maybe he was actually in the middle of emptying the contents of his intestines down the toilet. There was no way to be sure.

"Don't go making problems, Mr. White! Open this door!"

Mr. White opened the door soon afterward. I was kind of hoping they would have had to bust it down.

I never get anything I want.

Immediately after getting home, I jogged up the stairs and into the bedroom. My wife had just gotten out of the shower. I put my hands on her shoulders and squeezed tight. "Holy shit. I think our neighbor is a drug dealer."

"What are you talking about?"

"The dude is getting arrested right now. There are, like, twenty cops out there."

She didn't even dry off. She just wrapped a towel around herself, sprinted into the bedroom and pressed her face against the glass of the window.

Quicker than Mr. White's booty would later get plowed in prison, my wife and I were peeking through our upstairs blinds, watching the cops as they walked in and out of our neighbor's house. They were talking on walkie-talkies, and they were making notes, and they were doing all sorts of police mumbo jumbo. They even spent some time searching his SUV. They looked under the hood, and pulled back the seats, and climbed underneath it - the whole shebang.

About an hour and a half later, they left, without Mr. White.

Guess they didn't find what they were looking for. Or maybe they had the wrong house? Or maybe it really was me they were looking for all along?

Maybe I was going to get to bury my head in those triple-boobs after all.

Mr. White looked up at the house and spotted my wife and I peeking like perverts through the blinds. We shut them quickly, jumped into bed, and pulled the cover up and over us.

Guess I'll have to settle for just two boobs.

THIS THING GOES WHERE?

THIS THING GOES WHERE?

I'll be the first to admit that my wife and I aren't extremely adventurous when it comes to sex. There's not a lot of role-playing. There's certainly no sex outdoors and there aren't really any costumes. We've never done it in a car, or on a house, or with a mouse.

Don't get me wrong, we don't engage in the act of love like your grandparents, with crew cuts, pantyhose, and for the sole purpose of procreation. At the same time, you won't ever bump into us at a sex club downtown, then end up, literally "bumping" into us, an hour later back at your place over a bottle of wine.

I don't plan on growing a mustache anytime soon and neither of us have an interest in kimonos.

We like to keep it old school in the sack. You know, like Grandmaster Flash or Run DMC.

We're OG when it comes to lovin'.

Some years ago, I used to write a fairly popular blog on a site most people have forgotten called Myspace. One specific entry was titled "I Suck At Sexy Talk" and it was about a time in the sack in which I ruined what could have possibly been a *"sexy"* encounter with my wife, by showing her exactly the sort of dork she'd married by uttering the words "space age polymers" in the heat of the moment.

The very next day, I received an email from a long-time reader and a friend. It went something like this, "You know, if you want, I could send you guys this bondage tape stuff I have here at the house. It's cool stuff because it only sticks to itself and not to skin. Then you wouldn't have to worry about space age polymers."

As it turns out this reader/friend once sold sex toys.

Apparently, she wasn't very good at it, because she had a bunch of leftover items stashed in boxes throughout her house.

I told her to send over whatever she had.

You know, because I didn't want to be rude.

At the end of her email, she added in, "Oh, and I'll send you guys a little surprise as well."

Bondage tape and a surprise? And I'd get it all for free? And it wasn't even my birthday?

Everyone should have an online friend with poor sales skills.

A week or so later, the box arrived. With a smile on my face so wide it looked inhuman, I ran it upstairs and set it on the bed where my wife was sitting and reading a magazine.

I pulled out the tape and tried to flash a sexy look her way. It looked more creepy than sexy. I think the way my eyebrows were moving freaked her out. I tossed the tape to the side, flipped the box upside down, and out fell the *"surprise."*

Um.

I'm ashamed to say I had no idea what I was looking at.

I rubbed my chin and scratched my head. I squinted my eyes and sighed. I still didn't know what it was. I lifted it to the light and poked the plastic container with my finger.

I still had no idea.

What the hell did this crazy woman send me?

The device (for lack of a better word) was a clear gummy-looking thing. It was essentially a ribbed band that went all the way around a smaller ribbed band with a little motorized something or other dangling from the bottom. The whole thing was packaged in that annoying plastic that's impossible to open without a pair of scissors.

I had never been so confused in all my life.

I was holding it in the air, trying to figure out where it went and what it was used for when my wife chimed in. "What is it?"

"I'm not sure."

"Let me see it."

"Hold on a minute, I'm still looking."

She leaned forward and snatched it from my hand. She twisted it around and flipped it upside down. I think she was looking for instructions.

We were like a couple of Archaeologists that had just uncovered some confusing piece of pottery from prehistoric man. We were pawing at it, and trying to pry it open, and examining it from different angles and trying to connect the pervert dots in our mind. We looked like idiots.

Suddenly, a light goes off in my wife's head. She thought she'd figured it out. "I think it goes on the tongue."

I looked at the rubber and I looked at the black, mechanical vibrator thingy. *I wasn't putting that thing anywhere near my tongue.*

"What? You're nuts. It doesn't go on the tongue."

"Yes it does, Steven."

"You've lost your mind. It's a vibrator. If one of us sticks that thing on our tongue, it'll be the last thing we ever do."

After about twenty minutes of, arguably, the most bizarre conversation my wife and I had ever had, we finally figured out where the thing was supposed to go and how it was supposed to be used.

The smaller band stretched around the girth of the man's tubesteak while the larger band came down and snapped around the boys hanging below. The little vibrator bobbed around on the top and was supposed to stimulate the little man in the boat of the lady.

Wow. I really went out of my way to clean that up.

Why did I do that?

Suddenly, I'm a prude?

Let me remedy that.

Cock. Balls. Clit. Vibrate. *Wheeee!*

Easy enough to figure out, right? Well, it should have been. And it might have been for any two people other than us.

After we deciphered the riddle of our confusing gift, I asked the wife if she wanted to try it out, and I asked with a wide smile and bobbing eyebrows.

"Are you insane?"

I should really stop doing that with my eyebrows.

With the wife having no interest in adding strange, battery-operated gadgets sent from strangers into our lovemaking, I was forced to go it alone. I waited until she was gone the next day and cut it open. I had to. It was a gift. Someone took the time to package it, and address it and send it to me while asking for nothing at all in return.

I had to at least see how it fit.

It was the polite thing to do.

When I finally got the damn thing on, it was squeezing my boy so tight that he had not only doubled in girth, but fifty thousand veins that weren't there a moment before had magically appeared.

Basically, my penis transformed into the arm of a steroid abuser.

Stupid wife didn't know what she was missing.

I clicked on the vibrator thingy and suddenly the whole contraption started whirring and buzzing, and sending vibrations into my sack. It was slamming my balls together at an incredible rate.

Something popped, or twisted, or crunched. I think one of my nuts might have cracked.

You might not think that a testicle can crack, but I'm here to tell you that you're wrong about that.

They can crack.

Oh, boy can they crack.

When I tried to turn off the vibrator, I discovered the little knob was stuck. When I twisted harder, the damn thing began vibrating faster. Grunting in pain as my manhood cooked like a hotdog on the grill, I eventually managed to peel the hissing, burning *pleasure* machine from my dong and throw it across the room.

All in all, it wasn't very *pleasurable*.

In fact, it sort of sucked.

The next day I sent an email to my junk-burning Internet pal and told her that the damn thing nearly char-grilled my genitals. She seemed genuinely surprised and told me that one of two things must have been wrong.

1. I was wearing it wrong.

2. I had the absolute biggest penis of anyone she'd ever sold one of them to.

I was pretty confident that I was wearing it correctly so process of elimination meant…

Suddenly all the pain was worth it.

-Steven Novak-

PUT THIS KETCHUP ON YOUR FACE

PUT THIS KETCHUP ON YOUR FACE

I've always made things.

It's just what I do.

When I was a very young kid, I started my own line of homemade "Metal" dolls. I pieced them together with stapled pieces of fabric, bits of wood, and whatever I could scavenge from the garbage cans around the house. I had a Slash doll, one of Vince Neil, and even one for the lead singer of Cinderella - whose name I can't recall and barely even knew back then.

I didn't make versions of the Nelson twins. *No one liked the Nelson twins.* Even the Nelson twins didn't like the Nelson twins.

At one point, I opened a bug zoo with a friend of mine from school. My little brother and I opened a library where our family and neighbors could actually check out books and comics.

When the Garbage Pail Kids were all the rage, I thought it was too easy to simply collect them and made a hundred of my own.

I wrote an endless amount of books. I wrote and illustrated over 300 comic books.

I once tried to sell a homemade paper airplane instructional manual.

I participated in, and filmed, an endless amount of backyard wrestling.

I made my own board games, and constructed websites, and put together DVD's.

Over the years, I wrote, and filmed, no less than fourteen feature-length movies.

The list goes on, and on, and on, and on.

Want to hear something sad, though? *I still do most of it to this day.*

Want to hear an even sadder thing? *I managed to convince my younger brother and many of his friends to come along on nearly every venture.*

Want to hear the absolute saddest thing of all the sad things? *I think he enjoyed it almost as much as I did.*

Some years ago, I was scheduled to make a return trip to Illinois, in order to visit the family. It was summer, and I was only planning on staying a couple of days because that's all the time I could get off of work. Sure, it was going to be nice to see my mother again and finally getting to meet my brother's fiancée was certainly a plus, but the real thing that had me excited was the opportunity to get to film some scenes for a cross-country movie my brother and I were making.

Screw the family bullshit.

I had nonsense to make!

Minutes after arriving and seconds after being introduced to my brother's love interest, he said to me, "So, you wanna get some filming done?"

My mother looked annoyed. His girl looked surprised. Neither of us really gave a fart.

The nonsense wasn't going to make itself!

Over the years, I've learned that most human beings with vaginas and wombs, and other things I don't generally have interest in outside of the ways they might satisfy my selfish, sexual urges, don't really understand my desire to make stuff. Maybe that's because they're smarter than me. *I dunno.* I guess I sort of don't care.

I don't particularly understand purses, make-up, and vampires that sparkle.

To each their own, I suppose.

My brother jogged into the kitchen, opened the fridge and pulled out a bottle of ketchup. Then he turned to his new lady-friend. "Come here. I need to smear this on your face."

She looked at him like a load just dribbled from his pants leg and a puddle of poo juice was forming beneath his feet.

Ten minutes later, she was lying on her back in the woods with her head propped up on a spare tire and Heinz smeared across her confused face. There was a rock jabbed in her back.

She was clearly uncomfortable and she was trying to get my brother's attention. "My neck hurts…this tire is kind of hurting my neck."

My brother was messing with his camera. He was setting up a shot and only half heard her complaint. "It's okay. You'll be fine."

She looked at him like he'd just smeared his face into the poo puddle beneath his feet and slurped the lumpy nastiness into his mouth like it might be a bowl of soup.

Ten minutes later, she was tied to one of the posts on my mother's bed, screaming at my brother, in a faux alien voice, and trying her best to look *intimidating*.

She was failing, but she certainly earned points for being a good sport.

Confused about exactly what to say, she looked to me for advice. "Wait, what am I supposed to say?"

"Just say, 'you humans have destroyed this world, exhausted its resources, and now it's ours!' Oh, and try to make your voice sound a little more gruff."

"Huh?"

"I don't know. Give it some meanness."

"Huh?"

"You know, more evil."

I don't think she was overly impressed with my directorial abilities.

Twenty minutes later, and she was back outside, slowly approaching my ketchup-covered corpse sprawled out in the street when she noticed someone watching from a nearby window. "I think those people are watching us."

My brother and I were trying to settle on the best angle to shoot the scene. We barely heard her.

"Ya, people always do that."

It went on and on like this for a good two, maybe three, hours. We really put the poor girl through the paces. I don't know if she hated it or not. I mean, I imagine that she didn't think it was the most fun thing she'd done all week, but I don't think she wanted to kick us both in the nuts.

If she did, she never mentioned it.

She was probably a powder keg of annoyance just below the surface, though. Maybe she finally erupted the day after I left, tackled my brother to the ground, wedged some rocks into his back, kneeled on this neck and poured an entire bottle of ketchup onto his face before beating him with the empty plastic container.

She did end up marrying him - *so maybe not.*

I guess I couldn't have blamed her if it did.

The thing is, she needed to know what she was getting herself into.

If she was really in love with my brother, and she wanted to spend the rest of her life with him, and pop his kids from her vagina, she needed to understand that the moviemaking and all sorts of nonsense came with the territory.

In fact, I think it's in tiny little letters on the bottom of the second page of their marriage certificate. It's her fault if she didn't bother to read it carefully enough.

As long as I'm alive, I'm going to make shit. *It's what I do.*

As long as I'm alive, I'm going to be able to talk my brother into making shit with me. *It's also what I do.*

My advice? *Hire a hit man.* A good one.

And make sure he gives me two shots to the head and one to the belly.

I'm a tough son of a bitch to keep down.

-Steven Novak-

THEY'LL LET ANYONE SIT UP HERE

THEY'LL LET ANYONE SIT UP HERE

Quite some years ago, the self check-in machine at the airport asked me if I'd be interested in upgrading my seat to first class for a measly fifty bucks. Any other day of the week I would have chuckled at the absurdity of the idea, promptly touched the *"No Thank You"* button and headed to my gate content in the knowledge that I wasn't one of those pompous, first class flying douche bags that think they're better than everyone else and deserve special treatment. I'd get on the plane, cram my ever-widening backside into a coach seat between a big sweaty guy and a crying baby, content in the knowledge that I wasn't Paris Hilton, I didn't think I was hot shit, and I, certainly, didn't need to be pampered.

Pampering is for babies and men in their forties with weird sexual tendencies.

I was neither.

Plus, I would have saved myself fifty bucks - which I could then waste on that autographed picture of Levar Burton that I spotted on *eBay* a week prior.

If it's wrong for a grown man to have an autographed pictured of Geordi LaForge on the wall of his office instead of pictures of family and friends, then I don't want to be right.

For whatever reason, though, on this particular day in this particular airport, at this particular check-in kiosk, the fates conspired, the stars aligned, I was touched by the cosmic dance of the solar eclipse - or maybe God was just being a jerk. Whatever the case, instead of clicking *no thanks*, I clicked *yes*.

Yep, I was on my way to first class.

First class jerks! Kiss my ass you coach-traveling losers!

When the speaker called for first class travelers to board, I took a deep breath, stood and began to make my way to the jetway. I couldn't believe I was actually doing it. I was really going to fly first class!

Would I get to sit next to a movie star? No, wait - maybe a head of state? Would they offer me one of those goofy little drinks with umbrellas in them? Would the flight attendants be extra-busty and would that extra boob flesh be crammed into an extra small, extra low-cut top? Would they be flashing the sort of cleavage that makes a man want to go skiing?

Wow. I was really doing it. *First-damn-class.*

I felt like Latoya Jackson, or Kathy Griffin, or even Ben Vereen.

Okay, so maybe those examples sucked, but you get what I'm trying to say, right? Plus, I've always wanted to work an obscure reference, like Ben Vereen into a story and it's a heck of a lot harder to pull off than you might think.

When I stepped off the jetway and onto the plane boarding, the Flight Attendant took a look at my ticket, quickly exchanged the kind half-happy, half-annoyed smile she reserved for the coach passengers and replaced it with one more appropriate for a first class traveler like myself. "Welcome, Sir! I certainly hope you enjoy your flight!"

I was practically royalty. I half expected Pipa Middleton to strut past in a bikini.

For those of you who haven't yet had the opportunity to fly *first* (that's what all the hoity-toity firsters like myself call it), let me just say that the seats are pretty damn comfortable. They really are. They're wide and soft, and when you first plop your cheeks into them, they mold around your curves and softly caress your undercarriage like clouds sprinkled with warm molasses.

In fact, everything is more comfortable up there.

Everything is spacious and roomy, and safe and secure, and nothing smells like feet, or ass or feet-ass.

First class is sort of like returning to your mothers' womb - you know, minus the breathing in of womb-glop thing - unless you're flying Southwest, that is.

For the first hour of my flight, my first class experience was going perfectly, and this was odd, because things so rarely go perfectly for me. If history was any indication, something had to go wrong and something did.

Clunk. *Splash!*

The guy sitting beside me knocked his drink right into my lap.

Much better. Now it felt a lot more like my life.

Mr. ShitDrink quickly grabbed his tiny little napkin and began dabbing at my shirt. "O, geez. Shit. I'm sorry. Damn it, my hand just slipped..."

The instant his hand wandered awkwardly close to the bulge in my jeans I nudged it away.

I was covered in sticky booze, I was annoyed, and somehow I still managed to fight the urge to stick my thumbs in his eyes and push back until I hit brain. I kept things cool and I kept things civil. "Don't worry about it. It was an accident. No big deal. It happens."

God is like an annoying frat boy when it comes to me. I'm not sure why, but He seems to love tossing *zingers* my way - one after another – year after year. I bet He's up there right now, laughing His ass off, and relaxing on a recliner so comfortable it makes the seats in first class look like pointy rocks laced with the Bird Flu.

So God put his bucket of water above the door and it landed on me, and He got himself a nice little chuckle out of the whole thing. Unfortunately, He wasn't quite done.

Barely twenty minutes later, and Mr. Spills was sound asleep and snoring - loudly. His arm kept having these quick little spasms and his elbow was jabbing me in the chest and the neck.

Damn it.

I squeezed as close to the window as I could and suddenly he was only hitting my arms. While this was indeed an improvement, it was a marginal one, at best. I was still sticky and now I was bruised.

This sucked.

It sucked unwiped ass.

Ten minutes later, he started farting.

Some of them were long, some of them were short, some were barely there poppers, and some carried with them the ever so faint odor of the booze he actually managed to get down his gullet. They were coming non-stop. It was like he'd been holding in all the gas he'd ever had in his life and saving it for this single moment.

He was a beef machine.

The accumulated odor of a lifetime of gas was horrendous. It was moist and it was wet, and it was covering everything. It was sticking itself to the already stinky clothes, stacking itself like pancakes cooked up by a mental patient. It was everywhere at once, thick and inescapable. It was the morning dew on a foggy day, if the dew happened to be diarrhea and the fog a cloud of wrongfully digested burrito gas.

The couple in the seat across the aisle could hear it as well. They would chuckle each time one squirted out. I dug my iPod out of my carry-on, wedged the buds deep into my ears, turned the volume way up, pulled my shirt up and over my nose like a ninja and tried to keep from throwing up.

Joe EndlessFart woke up about thirty minutes later, spotted me wearing my iPod, and decided, for some reason, to start up a conversation. "Oh, are you a musician or something?"

Are you kidding me? An iPod equals musician?

Now I really wanted to punch this guy.

Not only did I want to smash him so hard in the gut that his insides popped from between his lips like cold spaghetti, I certainly didn't want to talk to him, or look at him, or be anywhere near him. I wanted out of his fart cloud, I wanted out of first class and I wanted off the plane.

Annoyed, I grumbled the word, "yes."

So what if it was a lie? I didn't care anymore. He'd ruined my shirt, his farts had undoubtedly ruined my sense of smell, but, most importantly, he'd utterly demolished my first class experience.

"Oh, yeah? Ever do anything I might have heard of? What's the name of your band?"

I said the first thing that popped into my head, "Weezer."

I figured it would give him a nice story to tell his buddies at the next company picnic: how he farted on the guy from Weezer.

DUCK STAIN

DUCK STAIN

There are times in a relationship when something so awful, and so disgusting and unforgettable occurs that it forever changes the way you look at your significant other from that day forth. No matter what you do, no matter how hard you might attempt to return things to the way they'd been, you fail. The wounds created are so very deep that the scar will remain, no matter how well it's stitched up.

My wife and I have experienced such an occurrence.

It was a few years ago, a Saturday night. We were watching television, *The Simpsons,* maybe? She was on the couch wearing only a long T-shirt, her sweatpants and a grin. I was on the floor in front of her wearing significantly more.

No, wait, we weren't watching *The Simpsons*. She was watching something stupid. *An awful lot of what she watches is stupid.*

I mean, seriously, *Dance Moms*? I'm not twelve or forty-three. I don't have a vagina. I don't think Beyonce is *hawt*. I don't think Justin Bieber is a dreamboat and I don't read weird young adult novels about teenage romance and fondly remember the days before my three children stepped on my dreams, leaving me with nothing but stretch marks and a c-section scar.

I shouldn't watch *Dance Moms*. Ever.

In every way, it was a very normal, very plain, Saturday night. There was, absolutely, nothing remarkable or memorable about it.

Until my wife started screaming. "Ohmygod! Ohmygod! Ohmygawd!"

At first, I didn't take her too seriously and I was in no rush to come to her aid. Keep in mind that this was a woman who, very literally, often shed tears at the sight of spiders. She would freeze up, drop to her knees, bury her head in her hands and cry until I squashed it

It was sad.

It also made it difficult to take her seriously.

"Ohmygod! Ohmygodsteven! Steven!"

She wasn't stopping and, because she wasn't stopping, I figured I should turn around and see just what all the fuss was about.

What's that? You broke a nail? *Oh, really?* You stubbed your toe? *Ouch?* Got a cramp in your leg? *Oh noes.* Hey, did I ever tell you about the time I got four hundred stitches in my head? Or, wait, how about the time three dudes beat the piss out of me while walking home from school? *No?* Old man had a go at me? Did I forget to mention that one? No worries, let me take a look at that stubbed toe, *sweetums*.

By the time I turned around, she was already up and running past me. She hurried through the kitchen, moving in the direction of the bathroom. Suddenly, I felt sort of bad. Something must have been really wrong with her. She had been sick for a few days prior to this moment. I probably should have taken that into consideration.

Terriblehusband strikes again.

"Ohhhhmmmyyyygooddd, Steven!" She was screaming at me from the bathroom.

I ran to her side. "What? What happened? Are you okay?"

She was on the toilet, sweating, hysterical, a pained expression on her face, tears running down her cheeks.

"Jeezus! What happened? Are you all right?"

I could see the hesitation in her eyes. She had something on her mind, something she dare not say. Something she wanted to keep a secret but knew she couldn't. When she finally spoke it was a whisper, shamed, her head hung low. "Don't look on the couch."

Of course, immediately, I wanted to look at the couch.

It was a natural reaction.

You'd have done the same.

Don't lie.

I headed back into the living room. Behind me I could hear her urging me to turn back, begging me to pretend the couch no longer existed.

I ignored her.

Moments later, I would wish I hadn't.

When I arrived at the couch, I finally got to see what had her so worked up.

One. *Entire.* Cushion. Was covered in dook.

It was mess. It was an atrocity. A massive brown stain extended from the center, stretching to each of the four edges and folding underneath. For some odd reason, I remember thinking it looked like a duck. It was an awful brown, wet, *shit-soaked* duck – like one of the animals after the Exxon disaster, only with poop.

The wife was screaming from the bathroom, "I told you not to look! Oh, no! I knew I was sick! I knew it! I told you not to look!" Her sentences were chopping, screamed from between diarrhea farts and the sickening sound of toilet water splashes.

I tried to turn my eyes from the couch, *I really did.* I was hypnotized. The voice of Daffy Duck wafted into my head. The stain was talking to me, speaking in a language only understood by poo stains everywhere.

A moment later, the smell hit me - like an outdoor toilet at a hippie camp ground, a garbage can filled with used tampons or a New York City subway - like Colin Farrell.

It traveled in through my nose, quickly moved to my brain and hit my frontal lobe with the force of Superman's punch.

As my wife sat on the toilet screaming for me to look away, I found myself heading for the other bathroom because I was going to say hello to the bowl of Coco Krispies I'd eaten earlier that day.

A great deal of time has passed since, what we still refer to as "The Couch Shitting Incident," took place.

It's a memory now, one we've both tried to forget and rarely bring up.

Sometimes, though, honestly, when she talks, all I hear is a *quack*.

I HATE MISSED OPPORTUNITIES

-Steven Novak-

I HATE MISSED OPPORTUNITIES

My wife is a nut.

She's nuttier than a squirrel rubbing a nut against the underside of its nut sack while munching on an Almond Joy.

She's nuttier than my poop after I've eaten a squirrel that was rubbing a nut on the underside of its nut sack while munching on an Almond Joy.

Everyone we've ever met seems to automatically assume that I'm the messed up weirdo in the relationship. While I wouldn't necessarily call them *wrong*, they aren't entirely right either.

The truth is that my wife is just a lot better at hiding her craziness when she is out in public. She actually cares what people think about her and she wants them to like her.

I don't.

Let me tell you something, though. When the lights go off, and when we're alone, and when it's just the two of us, the mask of normalcy fades away and all the weird, horrifying goodness she keeps inside comes out to play.

Scratch that. Replace the word "goodness" with "awfulness."

While you're at it, replace the word "play" with "confuse."

So what exactly is it that makes my wife so wacky-crazy-goofy-cuckoo? Lots of stuff. For the sake of keeping this story short, I'll focus on just one.

A while back, we were sitting in bed watching television when she leaned to me and said, "Steven, I think my esophagus is shifting."

It took my brain a minute to process that. "What?"

"I'm serious, Steven, it's shifting, or it's shrinking, or something. It's moving. I know it's moving. I can feel it moving."

I should have just ignored her. You can't debate with crazy and I shouldn't have tried. "I can guarantee, one-hundred percent, that the only thing your esophagus is doing is sitting inside your body, packed in tightly with a bunch of other gross bloody stuff."

"I don't know, Steven. I still think it's shifting. They can shift, you know."

"Pretty sure they can't."

"You don't know."

"Yes, I do."

Strangely enough, this wasn't even the first time she'd claimed that something like this was happening to her. Actually, it was almost a weekly thing.

"Steven, I think my wind pipe is closing shut."

"Steven! *Ohmygodohmygod*, I think my intestines are unraveling!"

"Steven, I think I need to see a doctor. My eyes keep moving backward. If they don't stop, they'll be pressed up against my brain!"

One time, I encouraged her to call the doctor and make an appointment. I also suggested that she be sure to explain, in great detail, just how her intestines were unraveling. She didn't do it.

I really wish she would have.

If I believed, for a second, that my wife was joking about any of this, she would undoubtedly be one of the most creative and original comedic minds since Andy Kaufman. She's not joking, though. When this nonsense rolls from her brain and sprays from her mouth, she's dead serious. With every ounce of her being, my wife legitimately believed her intestines were unraveling.

Where were they going, exactly?

I dunno.

Science, logic, and basic common sense are meaningless when my wife gets something in her head.

Not too long ago, we were on our way home from a quick trip to a local grocery store when a sudden gust of wind sent a cardboard box flying directly in the path of our car.

She basically freaked the hell out.

She screamed at the top of her lungs, jerked the wheel violently to the side, nearly slamming us into the car in the next lane over and driving us off the road, at the same time. The worst part of it is that all of her screaming and jerking accomplished nothing. My head cracked off the passenger side window and we still ran over the box.

We smashed that thing, spit it out behind us and tossed it into the air.

Okay, so maybe it surprised her and caught her by surprise. *Whatever.* Her reaction was silly, but whatever. It was over. She'd survived the dreaded cardboard box and we were continuing on our merry way.

No, we weren't.

Her entire body was shivering. Her lips were quivering. Her ears were smivering and her feet were plivering.

Okay, so I made those last two words up. So what? *What of it?* I wanted to rhyme something with shivering and quivering. I thought it would be fun. Sue me.

Besides, you know you laughed at *smivering*.

Admit it.

Thick, wet tears began rolling down her cheeks. Her breathing was all messed up. She was only half inhaling. The other half was a whimper. She was crying like a puppy being scolded for pissing on the living room carpet.

A part of me felt bad for her. Another part was confused. "It's okay. Hey, what are you crying for?"

Spit rolled down her chin. Runny make-up dripped from her cheek. "I-I-I-ju-I-jus-just..."

"You just what? Maybe you should pull over, hun."

"N-no. I-just-I-that bo-that box..."

I put my hand on her shoulder and massaged gently. "It was just a box. Relax. All you did was run over a box. Take it easy and try to breathe"

"The-there was a baby in that box, wasn't there?"

I stopped rubbing.

"I ju-ju-just know there was a baby in that box..."

This nutcase didn't deserve my rubs.

"What the hell are you talking about?"

"Th-that's what they do, Steven! They put babies in boxes and they leave them in the street. That's what they do!"

Who were "they?"

Where were "they" doing this?

Why were "they" doing this?

Did "they" do this often?

Once again, *I dunno.*

I should have just told her that she had, indeed, run over a baby in a cardboard box - a baby so light that it dipped and bobbed in the breeze before rolling underneath our tires - a baby so thin that it was able to fit inside a collapsed cardboard box.

I should have let her believe she had murdered an infant.

I should have, but I didn't.

Damn it.

I hate missed opportunities.

Goats Eat Cans Volume 3

WHERE'S THE CAR?

WHERE'S THE CAR?

When I opened the door to the garage, I noticed my car was missing.

That didn't seem right.

Unsure if I'd really seen what I thought I'd seen, I stepped back into the kitchen and took a moment to collect myself. My car shouldn't have been missing. It was there when I went to bed the day before, *wasn't it?* Sure it was. Where else would it be? It was there the night before and logic dictated that it had to be there the morning after.

Oprah's Cable Channel was a joke, Whitney Houston liked her booze, Joan Rivers had seven blobs of ass putty masquerading as a face, and my car was in the garage. Those were constants. They would never change. They could be counted on.

The fact that my car was in the garage was a constant, too. It had to be.

My wife was home. She was sitting in the bedroom putzing around with her computer and her car was in the garage, exactly where it was supposed to be.

I'd seen it.

At least, I thought I'd seen it.

It was right there.

At least, I thought it was right there.

No, my car had to be in the garage. The garage door was closed. Nothing was broken into. I wasn't stepping on shattered glass or splinters from an exploded window frame. Late night intruders hadn't beaten me at some point during the previous eight hours and my backside felt mostly un-raped. My car had to be there. *It had to.*

I stepped back into the garage.

My car still wasn't there.

Shit.

Where the hell was my car?

My first thought was that I needed to, somehow, keep the knowledge of my disappearing automobile from my wife. I wasn't entirely sure what was going on, but I was also keenly aware of the fact that it was more than likely my fault. And if it was my fault, she wasn't going to be happy.

Why would she be? Apparently, I'd lost the car.

If the shoe had been on the other foot and she'd somehow lost the car, I would have been pissed. I might have been so pissed that I pissed myself.

Maybe I could blame it on her?

No, that wasn't going to work.

I was the last one to drive my car and now my car was gone. *This was not good.*

I strolled into the garage and touched the area where it should have been on the off chance that it turned invisible. It hadn't turned invisible – which meant David Copperfield and Wonder Woman were no longer persons of interest.

Damn it. A part of me was looking forward to frisking Wonder Woman.

I spent the next fifteen minutes pacing around the kitchen trying to replay the events of the previous day in my head. I clearly remembered driving the car to the store and driving it home again.

That was it. That was all I'd done. That was the only place I went and the only time I drove the stupid-*fucking*-thing. *So, where the hell was my car?* Why wasn't it in the garage where it was supposed to be?

Maybe I needed to frisk Wonder Woman just to be sure? Maybe tweak her nippl… "Steven? Can you bring me a glass of water?"

Damn it, shit.

The wife was calling me from the other room. What the hell was I going to tell her? My palms turned from dry to damp in the blink of an eye. My foot began to tap anxiously on the tile; I was nibbling on my nails. I ran my fingers through my hair and, suddenly, I looked like Ted Kaczynski after a long weekend of letter writing. She was going to notice something was wrong. If I brought her that glass of water, she was going to notice something was wrong and I was going to have to tell her exactly what was wrong. *Shit. Damn. Shit. Gah!*

"Steven? Did you hear me?"

When I poured her a glass, it spilled onto the countertop. When I carried the glass to the bedroom, it spilled onto the floor. When I handed it to her, it spilled onto the bed. By the time she lifted it to her mouth, it was pretty much empty.

She shot me an angry glance and flipped the damp fabric off her lap. "What's the matter with you?"

"Nothing."

She could tell something was up. It was obvious something was up. I kept glancing in the direction of the garage. I was scratching my head, then scratching my ass and scratching my head again.

The ass scratches had nothing to do with the head scratches. *My butt just itched.*

"Seriously, Steven. Why are you acting so weird?"

I needed to tell her. If I couldn't figure out where the car was, I was going to have to call the cops and, at that point, the jig would, pretty much, be up. I was just delaying the inevitable. I didn't want to tell her, but knew I needed to tell her.

Honesty is important in a marriage, right? Even when you lose a car? *No?*

"The car's missing."

It took her a while to respond and when she finally did, she did it without punching me in the face, stomach, or groin. This caught me by surprise. "What?"

"It's not in the garage."

"Then where is it?"

I shrugged. *I probably shouldn't have shrugged.* She didn't seem to appreciate the shrug.

"You drove it last! Where is it?"

I almost shrugged again, but managed to catch myself. "I know I drove it last. Don't you think I know I drove it last?"

She made a fist. I think I heard her knuckles crack. I needed to come up with something more substantial than a shrug. A groin punch was coming and the stomach punch was a likely follow-up. Her jaw locked. Her upper lip began to twitch. "Steven, what did you do with our car?"

"I don't know. I drove it to th…" That's when it hit me. "Oh, shit."

"What?"

"I think I left it at the store."

She didn't respond. She didn't really need to. The look on her face, pretty much, said it all. She was staring at me like I'd just professed my love for Justin Bieber and whipped out a secret stash of posters, buttons and a teensy pair of too-small boxers I'd been hiding in the closet. She was staring at me like I just told her I wanted to shave the pubes from my crotch, spray paint them gray, glue them to my chin and start referring to myself as Gandalf the dickface. I didn't want her staring at me, anymore.

I grabbed my coat and my keys, and headed for the front door. "I'll be back."

Again, she said nothing. I didn't really give her an opportunity.

I'm guessing a part of her hoped I was lying – *about coming back, I mean.*

At the time, we lived just a few blocks from a little strip mall sort of thing, with a Staples, a Grocery store, a Starbucks and a bunch of other stuff. It was within walking distance and I had, in fact, walked to and from it quite a lot over the years. On a normal day, it would have taken me ten minutes to get there. On this particular morning ,it took just three.

Out of breath, I jogged to the Staples, stopped, scanned the parking lot, and there it was – right where I left it.

Yep, apparently I'd driven the car to the store the day before, bought what I needed to buy and then decided to walk home without a care in the world.

Apparently, I'm an idiot.

My wife looked at me differently for the remainder of the day. When my back was turned, I could feel her eyeballs on me – judging me – struggling to come to terms with the reality of whom she'd chosen to marry. With one stupid mistake, I'd transformed myself into an episode of *Perfect Strangers*, circa 1987. I was the screwball neighbor. I was the idiot comic relief. I was Woody from *Cheers*, and Steven Erkel, and Rose Nylund all rolled into one.

Two weeks later, I did it again.

The woman either has zero self-esteem or my penis is a heck of a lot more impressive than I think it is.

-Steven Novak-

WORST. TOAST. EVER.

WORST. TOAST. EVER.

"Have you thought about what you're going to say?"

"Maybe you should write a few things down for your brother's toast?"

"You know, you really should start thinking about what you're going to say for your brother's toast."

"Have you thought about it yet? The toast? You should be thinking about the toast."

"You should write that toast down. You don't want to look silly."

For weeks, this was the kind of stuff I heard.

It should be known that I am, for all intents and purposes, an anti-social. I get weird in large groups of people. I can't help it. I've been that way for a very long time. I know that the people trying to convince me that it was in my best interest to go into the toast at my little brother's wedding prepared were only trying to help. I understood this.

Honestly, though, I just wanted everyone to shut the hell up about it.

They were trying to help, but they weren't.

In fact, they were only making things worse.

The best one came from my mother on the night before the wedding. "You know, Steven, there are going to be like, a hundred and fifty people there. If you mess up that toast, you're messing up in front of two-hundred people."

The number of guests jumped from one hundred and fifty to two hundred over the course of her sentence.

Fantastic.

Thanks a lot.

That helps a ton, mom.

Now, sashay over here, spread just a little and let me kick you in the very same baby maker that spit my ugly ass out.

Despite my better judgment, I convinced myself, long beforehand, that I wasn't going to plan anything out. Nope. I was just going to let it flow. I wanted to shoot from the hip. Whatever was going to come from my mouth was going to come from my mouth for better or worse. Common sense could eat my nuts. I wanted to buck the trend. I wanted to do things my own way, damn it!

Common sense and good judgment never did anything for me anyway. *Screw 'em both. Screw 'em both right in the pooter!*

Not even in a good "I'm a homosexual, or a dirty, dirty girl and I happen to like it up the backside" sort of way, either.

Nope. I was going to screw them both in a "nasty, stinky, sweaty, rape followed by years of therapy and inevitable suicide" sort of way.

This is how I looked at the situation of the toast at my little brother's wedding.

Well, that's how I looked at it, right until the annoyingly, *peppy-cool* DJ handed me the mic, and announced to the room that the Best Man had "a little something he'd like to say."

In that instant everything changed.

The DJ with the soul patch had it wrong. The Best Man actually had a little something he was *supposed* to say when, in reality, he actually wanted to crawl into the broom closet, cry, and possibly make out with the mop.

The minute that spiky-haired dildo handed me the mic, I cursed myself for not listening to everyone who told me to plan something out beforehand.

My throat tightened up. My legs felt like two chubby pieces of spaghetti. They no longer had any interest in keeping me upright. My penis shrunk to toddler size. My heart sputtered and spit like the lungs of a fifty-year-old smoker, and the world started to blur.

Staring out into a distorted sea of well-dressed, slightly buzzed partygoers, I froze. "Um."

Everyone was looking at me. "Hm."

I could feel their eyes on my body. I could feel the goo from their pupils sliding across my skin. My hands were so saturated that the microphone almost slipped through my fingers.

I nervously tapped the top of it.

My brother looked up at me with his bride right behind him. They were waiting for me to say something. They were waiting for me to say anything. Instead, I was standing there like an idiot, perspiration pouring off me in buckets and my neck turning to rubber.

"Um. Okay. Well, I'll, um." I was failing hard. "I'll try and make this quick, because any of you who know me, know that the very fact that I'm even standing up here doing this is, well, it's, um…it's about as rare as a White Rhino."

Yep, I brought up a White Rhino.

I was failing really hard.

I brought up a White Rhino in my brother's wedding toast. A White Rhino? Seriously? That's the sort of thing that came from my mouth? I really thought that was a good way to get started.

White Rhino was my ice-breaker?

I wanted to slam my face into the table. It was a wedding toast and I was treating it like an episode of Mystery Science Theater! What was next, a reference to Manos: The Hands of Fate?

I lowered my head and told myself to, *"getbackontrack, getbackontrack, getyourassbackontrack."*

My legs were all but useless. I put my hand on my brother's shoulder to keep from passing out and toppling into his lap. "My brother, this guy right here. This guy you're looking at right now. Well, this guy right here was a friend to me, well, when I really had no friends…"

Oh, sweet lord.

I'd gone from White Rhino's to therapy sessions.

My voice cracked just a bit at the end of the sentence. My eyes began to water.

Oh, damn it.

Was I really going to start crying? *What the tit?* You've got to be *fucking* kidding me!

I told myself that I was going to drag myself into the bathroom the moment this debacle ended, give myself a swirly and then proceed to beat the shit out of myself like the guys in high school used to do.

I should have stopped, but I didn't. My mouth just kept on talking. My brain was already in the car and headed home. "Let me just say this…there are a whole lot of people here today who are happy for the both of you. But, um. Well, there are maybe only three or four of them happier for you than I am."

A particularly large, particularly salty bead of sweat dripped down my forehead, over my cheek, and into my mouth. Another followed it, and, soon enough, I was swallowing back my bodily fluids by the gallon.

Was I really sweating that much? I couldn't believe I was sweating that much! If I had taken off my jacket, it would have sprayed from me like a fire hydrant. It would have knocked over tables with tsunami-like force, swallowing the banquet room and drowning everyone in my gross, salty B.O. funk.

It would have been worse than Katrina. The government's response would have been slow. Kanye West would have appeared on MTV and let the world know.

My mind was rambling. I was thinking about Kanye West when I really needed to wrap up my utter failure of a speech and run screaming into traffic. "So, Um. I guess I could say good luck, but well, I've got a feeling that you won't need it. Instead, I'll just say congratulations."

Talk about your lame ass closing lines.

That was just sad. It might not have been as pathetic as my White Rhino drop, but it was certainly up there.

My brother stood up and gave me a hug. I awkwardly gave one to his new wife, Laura, as well; leaving her dress covered in sweat, and handed the microphone over to the Maid of Honor.

I sat down and buried my head in my hands, content in the knowledge that I'd just delivered the worst wedding toast in the history of wedding toasts.

I, totally, fucked it up.

Stupid loser - stupid, faux-hawk sporting loser.

Loser. Loser. Loser.

The Maid of Honor pulled out a piece of paper, unfolded it and settled into reading her toast in the most monotone, boring, droning voice I'd ever heard.

She rambled on for ten minutes. She was a train wreck. She was horrible. It was like she didn't know people were listening, or she simply didn't care. Her jokes fell flatter than a Thai girl's chest. Her emotional stuff packed as much punch as a very special episode of *Family Ties*.

I suddenly felt much better.

WHEN THE WIFE'S AWAY

WHEN THE WIFE'S AWAY

When my wife flew to Wisconsin, for nearly a month, to visit her son and her newborn granddaughter, things started getting weird around the house. You see, I don't have much of a life outside of my wife. My universe centers around her and, with her gone, I found myself doing more and more things that I shouldn't be doing.

No, no, no…not anything *bad*.

Get your mind out of the gutter.

I wasn't cheating on her, and I didn't start smoking crack, or stealing cars, or stealing cars while smoking crack and cheating on her.

I just did a lot of weird stuff – the sort of stuff grown men shouldn't be doing and the sort of stuff that's usually done to the *"special people"* in the *"special homes."*

At this point, I'm guessing that you're asking yourself just what in the world I'm talking about. If I'm not cheating on my wife, experimenting with drugs, or surfing the web for videos of women having sex with dogs, then what the hell was I doing?

Maybe I should just take you through an average day without my wife.

How about that?

You okay with that?

I don't care if you're okay with it.

Here it comes:

6:00AM: I woke up without the aid of an alarm clock, screaming kid, or rooster. I was in the middle of a sex dream that involved me gettin' busy with six women of varying race, hair color, accent, and boob size.

Oh, I guess I should mention that one of them was an Orion Slave Girl from the original *Star Trek* series.

Here's a little inside information: Orion cooch tastes like a bag of Fritos and feels like a bag of Fritos as well. *Go figure.*

Needless to say, the dream was pretty hot. I tried to go back to sleep and get right back into those green Frito folds, but I ended up dreaming about Michael Landon from *Little House on the Prairie*, instead. Needless to say, it wasn't all that hot.

Also, here's another smidge of inside information: the interior walls of Pa Ingalls' tush feels a lot like a bag of Fritos.

6:30AM: Sick of Pa's booty and his know-it-all lessons about the importance of family, I forced myself to get out of bed.

6:40AM to 5:00PM: Straight up, nose to the grindstone, work. I was driven and I was focused, and I was productive. I was a damn graphic designing dynamo! Pa Ingalls and his Frito butt had ruined my morning, but suddenly things were looking up!

5:30PM: I put the work aside and opted to eat some dinner. On the menu was a microwaveable Lean Cuisine meal - Chicken Alfredo, to be specific. It sort of tasted like crap, but at least it didn't taste like Fritos and I was far too lazy to actually cook anything of substance. I settled for crap and never looked back.

6:00PM: I, somehow, ended up sprawled on my back on the floor of my office. Scattered across the carpet beside me were G.I. Joe figures. I'd pick them up two at a time and have them fight each other on my chest - complete with sound effects for punches and explosions.

Not to brag or anything, but I do a hell of an explosion sound effect.

Seriously, you'd think shit was exploding all around you.

Flint beat Croc Master and moved onto round two where he'd take on the winner of Outback and Destro.

That was going to be a hell of a match.

7:00PM: The G.I. Joe Death Tournament reached a dramatic conclusion with Outback walking away with the title. I was tempted to start a new tournament using my horror movie action figures, but decided, instead, to move onto something else.

Freddy Kruger would have won anyway.

7:20PM: I tried getting back to work, but ended up drawing a goat giving a blowjob to a farmer while a Cirque de sole clown masturbated in a pig troth in the background.

This disturbed me.

I decided to move onto something else.

8:00PM: I somehow ended up in the bedroom painting my toenails black. Impressed with my painting abilities, considering the fact that I was a relative novice, I decided to paint my fingernails as well.

I was actually pretty good at it.

If I were gay or an Asian woman, I might have considered a career change.

8:40PM: I made the decision to watch every single hour of every single *Star Trek* series that I have on DVD in chronological order. It was going to be awesome and I couldn't believe I hadn't thought of it sooner!

8:50PM: After a not-so-extensive search, I managed to find a *Star Trek* time-line online so I wouldn't watch anything out of order. I was a boy scout once. *Preparedness is important.*

10:20PM: After only two episodes of *Enterprise*, I called it quits for the day and told myself that I would pick up where I left off in the morning.

Or maybe I'd just skip *Enterprise* all together as it was a fairly terrible show.

10:30PM: I forced myself back at my drawing table, and decided that I needed to get refocused when it came to work. There was still time to get the momentum back. I had to get focused. I could do this!

It was go time, bitch! *It was time to get serious!*

11:00PM: My momentum a thing of the past, I somehow found myself pencil-deep in part two, in my series of farmer sex drawings. This time, the old codger was sliding into his goat's pooter, while the Cirque de sole clown worked a broom up his own ass on a fence near the barn. The farmer's wife was in the house, crying on the phone with the police.

It was a pretty good rendering, despite its saucy subject matter. The goat-butt was spot-on.

I was pretty proud of it.

11:40PM: I would spend the next twenty minutes picking lint out of my belly button and smelling my finger. It stank like the underside of a Frito-crusted goat rectum.

12:00AM: I realized that I forgot to workout earlier in the day. I blamed Flint and the rest of the Joes.

12:10AM: I started watching an old 80's flick called *Silent Rage* with Chuck Norris as a local Sheriff who takes on a crazy man that's been given super-powers by a couple of scientists.

Despite not one, but two, sex scenes with Chuck, the movie proved better than expected. Double Norris-sex is one too many Norris sexes for me. Maybe it's the fire-red chest hair that makes it all seem so unsettling?

Further research was required.

1:40AM: For some reason, after spotting a bottle of Elmer's glue on my drawing table, I decided to squirt it onto my hands and let it dry. Once dry, I spent the next forty minutes picking it off and laughing to myself like a lunatic.

2:15AM: I washed my hands and decided to call it a night. The bed was calling my name and I could almost smell the promise of Slave Girl crotch in the air.

4:15AM: I woke up from a horrible nightmare that featured Chuck Norris getting head from a goat.

I decided not to go back to sleep.

MEET ME IN THE WOODS

MEET ME IN THE WOODS

My mother has been married twice and both of those marriages lasted around fifteen years - give or take. Her first husband, who also happened to be my father, was a very *man's man* sort of man. He was the kind of guy who liked working on cars and hammering nails into various pieces of wood. He mostly wore steel-toed boots and his hands were always covered in grease. He smelled like sawdust, and two-dollar steak, and anger stewed in frustration.

What's that? You think *anger* isn't really a smell?

You've never smelled my old man.

Remember when Christian Bale went off on that cameraman and the tapes were leaked to the Internet?

It smells exactly like that sounded.

Her second husband had almost nothing in common with the first. I'm not entirely sure that he even knew how to pop the hood of his car, and the only thing he ever hammered a nail into was his finger. Instead of steel-toed boots, he preferred a pair of slightly feminine loafers *(the ones with the little tassels)*. His hands were baby-smooth. He smelled like overpriced cologne, and filet mignon, and the possibility of "experimenting" in college.

That's a smell too. Trust me, on this one.

It smells an awful lot like Prince's motorcycle from Purple Rain.

While I spent my youth mostly terrified of my actual father, I don't recall ever once being intimidated by my stepfather. He was too quiet. He never said much and he kept to himself. On the rare occasions that he actually spoke up, it was usually to say something mostly corny.

Plus, he was significantly shorter and lighter than I was. He wasn't a tiny man, but he didn't exactly cast a long shadow either. I always felt like I could easily scoop him into my arms, carry him upstairs, tuck him into bed and kiss him on his terribly dated 1970's mustache.

It's difficult to be intimidated by anyone with a mustache.

Even if he couldn't beat his way out of a piss-soaked bag that had already been beaten out of by a more brawny man, mustache Glen was actually a pretty decent guy.

I know from experience that the role of a stepfather is not easily defined. Too many stepfathers overstep their bounds and push when they should just hang back. Glen never overstepped with me. He never wronged my brother or myself, and, to the best of my knowledge, the same could be said for his relationship with my mother.

Everything changed when she said she filed for a divorce.

At that point, mustache Glen went mustache nuts. And mustache nuts is twice as bad as regular nuts, so you know I'm talking about some serious-ass nuts here.

I suppose I should have seen it coming. It's always the quiet ones – *as my wife will discover when she eventually tries to divorce me.*

A month or so after my mother informed me of the impending end to her marriage, and a couple weeks after Glen had moved out of the house and into an apartment on the other side of town, my mother called me to say that the neighbors spotted him peeking through the windows in the middle of the day.

At this point, she already had a restraining order against him. Apparently, he would pull into the cul-de-sac every day, sit in his car at the end of the block and stare.

When I say, "stare" I mean, *"just stare."*

That's all he would do. For hours.

"What was he doing peeking in the windows?"

"I don't know, Steven. Janice just said she saw him pull into the driveway, run from his car and go from one window to the next for almost twenty minutes."

"That's weird."

"I talked to someone he works with, and apparently he hasn't been showing up to work either."

"Huh."

It was difficult for me to picture Glen doing any of that. The mustache Glen I'd known since seventh grade had always been so prim and proper. The man carried a tiny comb in his back pocket for emergency hair/mustache touch-ups.

I mean, come on. Mimi-comb guys who wear nothing but Dockers and button up shirts don't just go crazy. Crazy people and celebrities go crazy. Postal workers go crazy. Weird men in their early thirties who write three humor books focusing on the mostly awful moments of their lives go crazy.

Wait.

Anyway, Glen's sudden ticket for the crazy train didn't make sense to me.

Every week, my mother would call and offer up some bizarre new tale of my former stepfather's descent into madness.

One week, he pulled all the money from the bank and attempted to transfer it to another account. The next week, he spent the day going from house to house in the neighborhood, quizzing neighbors about how my mother was spending her days. The following week, she noticed him tailing her around town. Apparently, he was wearing dark glasses and, possibly, the first hoodie he'd worn in his life. Four days later, he began leaving five-minute rants in the voicemail of her cell phone.

Not only had he boarded the aforementioned crazy train, but the dude was wearing a conductor hat and had his foot pressed firmly on the gas.

I wanted to ask my mother if his mustache had grown all wild and unkempt - if it was a foot long and there were bugs and bits of salted deli meats coiled in the follicles like flies in a spider web.

I never did, but I always wanted to.

I bet it was, though.

That's how I pictured him, anyway.

Glen's mustache-divorce craziness reached a fevered pitch when my mother told me that he called her late one afternoon and suggested that they *"meet in the woods"* to work it out.

Meet in the woods, huh?

Yeah, I told her she probably shouldn't meet him in the woods.

If there's one thing I've learned in my time on this planet, it's that nothing gets *worked out* in the woods. The woods are where hillfolk go to rape and psychotics go to bury the post-raped dead.

The man would have fed her to his mustache and I'd have never heard from her again.

To this day, I don't know what in the world my mother could have done to drive, what seemed like a reasonably sensible man, to the point where he was inviting people to the woods for a late-night rendezvous.

Come to think of it, my father went bat-shit bonkers after she divorced him too.

Ew.

The woman must be a dynamo in the sack.

Double ew.

Goats Eat Cans Volume 3

THE RAPIST HOODIE

THE RAPIST HOODIE

"Steven, please take that thing off."

"What? What thing?"

"That hoodie. You can't go running in that hoodie."

What the hell was my wife talking about? What was wrong with my hoodie? I twisted my body and looked over my shoulder. Everything seemed normal to me. Better than normal. Everything seemed awesome.

I look pretty cool in a hoodie.

"Huh? Did I spill something on it?" I checked the sleeves and found an ittty bitty piece of smudtz. It was barely noticeable. She couldn't have been referring to the smudtz. The smudtz wasn't worth mentioning. No one was going to notice the smudtz.

(I should really stop typing the word smudtz. It's not even a real word.)

"You just can't wear it…at least not with the hood on. If you're going to go running in it, you have to take the hood off."

"No way. It's cold outside."

"Then you can't wear it."

The nerve of this broad.

"I still don't see what the problem is."

She sighed and shook her head. "You look like a rapist in that thing! You can't go running around in the middle of the night with a hood over your head! That's what rapists do, Steven!"

Rapists? *Seriously?* If I had two hoodies, I would have worn them both.

Not only was she trying to tell me – by all indications a grown-ass man – what I could and couldn't wear, but she was saying that I looked like a rapist, to boot.

I'd never seen them before, which surprised me, but apparently she had a massive set of balls.

I wasn't having it. I was going to wear my hoodie and that was that. Hell, if I had three hoodies I would have worn all three. Four of them, same deal. If there had been a hoodie store nearby, I would have jogged there, purchased seven more and ran home while crammed into all eleven.

If I could have, I would have worn all the hoodies in the world and started sewing some more for later that evening.

Oh, yeah, I was wearing the hoodie, damn it.

I returned the hood to my head. "You're nuts. No one is going to think I'm a rapist. It's 9:00 at night, anyway. There's not even anyone else out there." I grabbed onto the dangling strings and pulled it tight, grit my teeth and nodded defiantly, "I'm wearing the hoodie."

Without another word, I headed for the door.

Rapist? What was she talking about? I didn't look like a rapist. What was a rapist supposed to look like, anyway? Rapists didn't have a specific sort of look. Rapists looked like Roman Polanski and

Kobe Bryant and everything in-between. *(Which is, literally, almost everything.)*

Rapist, my ass.

Ouch.

The stiff chill of the California night hit my face the moment I stepped outside. I clicked on my iPod, kicked my legs, and I was off to the races. The further I ran, the further my wife and her hoodie-hate disappeared. I was focused on my feet and the task at hand.

You see, at the time I was working hard to get back into the shape of something more closely resembling a human being. A few years prior, I'd lost nearly all of my freelance clients in the span of a month. The economy was in the toilet and decent-paying work was particularly hard to come by, for a stretch. My ego took a hit. It shriveled like an Eskimo dong and a yearlong depression set in.

During that year, I grew very *roundish*.

My penis disappeared beneath the shadow of my expanding belly, my chin was reunited with a couple of long lost siblings, and the ghost of Neil Armstrong planted a haunted version of the Lunar Module into one of the many craters that had formed on my ass.

Getting back into shape was a priority.

In a desperate attempt to keep myself from getting winded when I took out the trash, I'd settled into the daily routine of a late-night jog. They were late-night jogs rather than early morning or middle of the day jogs because I figured there was less of a chance anyone would actually see me jogging at 9PM.

No one needed to see me jogging. *I didn't even want to see me jogging.* When I jogged, there were more things moving than just my legs, moving in every direction at once, gyrating and flopping.

I looked like a three-legged elephant with a nasty case of asthma and a couple of bum knees.

My jog/walk/heaving as chest pain crippled my body was a sloppy-painful two miles uphill and an awkward, slightly less painful, trip back down. On this night in particular, the journey up had been mostly standard fare. Five minutes in, I wanted to die. My legs were on fire. My legs were seconds from buckling, and I was fairly certain that my lungs had exploded. When I reached the halfway point, my hands fell to my knees and a partially digested wad of orange chicken and soy sauce sprinkled bile shot from my stomach and into my mouth.

Word of advice: never gorge yourself on Panda Express hours before you set out on a four-mile jaunt.

Panda Express tastes even worse the second time around.

In fact, just skip the damn Panda Express all together.

As terrible as I felt, and as awful as my second serving of Chinese food tasted, it did feel good to be out of the house and in the fresh air. Strangely enough, I'd actually begun to like my late-night excursions. It was dark. It was quiet. The breeze was crisp and most of the neighborhood was tucked away for the evening.

Best of all, no one other than myself could hear the fact that "Eye Of The Tiger" was embarrassingly blasting into my eardrums.

Don't judge me, you judgy son of a bitch.

So what if that's as predictable a workout choice as a Stephenie Meyer book is terrible?

I like to pretend I'm Clubber Lang when I'm running, and Mr. T when I'm not. It's just something I do.

Once I had my wind back, I began the second leg of my journey. A few minutes in, I spotted a bobbing light a hundred or so yards away. While it was rare for me to come across someone else so late in the afternoon, on the few occasions I did, they were, almost always, carrying a flashlight, or wearing reflectors or something.

They wanted people to see them and they wanted to stay safe. *Psh.*

I went the opposite way. I didn't want anyone to see me. I was dressed in black and I was a ninja. *Aw, yeah.*

Actually, at the time, I was more like the ninja that ate the other ninja's in his dojo, but that's neither here nor there.

It didn't take long for my safety conscious pal to get closer. When the light was fifty or so feet away, it suddenly stopped bouncing and I was able to vaguely make out the shape of the person holding it: a woman.

She was frozen in place. She could see me – or, at least she could, sort of, see me.

I probably looked like a super massive black hole, wiggling and wobbling like the ghost of Fatty Arbuckle against the moonlight from her perspective, but she seemed fairly certain that *something* was lumbering in her direction, huffing like a hippo in heat, begging to be mounted.

When I was ten feet away, her eyes went wide and her mouth dropped. In a single, not so fluid movement, she hopped over the bushes, bolted for the other side of the street and didn't stop until her feet hit the sidewalk.

This was pretty awkward.

So maybe it was a rapist hoodie.

Seemed like a bit of an overreaction on her part, though.

I never told my wife what happened, but I never stopped wearing the hoodie, either.

I'm not entirely sure what either of those things say about me.

-Steven Novak-

SPIDERS IN THE CABIN

SPIDERS IN THE CABIN

"Ohmygawd! Steven! OhmygawdOhmygawdOhmygawd!"

It was one in the morning and my wife had just leapt from the bed and was currently hopping around the room with tears in her eyes, her arms flapping like a baby bird attempting to fly for the very first time.

At least, I think it was one in the morning – I was just barely awake, after all.

Before I could find out what was wrong, my wife tore open the bedroom door and ran into the hallway. I swear to God, I'd never seen her move so fast. Her ass was spring loaded. She left a puff of smoke behind and a cartoonish trail of fire on the floor.

Until that point in our marriage, I had absolutely no idea I was banging Usain Bolt. I had even less of an idea that he was a half Mexican southern California woman without a penis.

Go figure.

I eventually caught up with the wife in the living room. She was cowering in the corner, wide-eyed, staring at the floor and nervously biting her fingernails. When I tried to touch her, she socked me in the chest.

"What the hell is wrong?!"

"There was a spider! There was a spider on me!"

Oh, sweet lord. *Are you fucking kidding me?*

She was acting like someone had attacked her with a chainsaw, or at the very least, a grossly oversized machete of some sort. This was all because of a spider? A spider? The spazzing, jumbled mess of a human being darting between both the flight and fights instincts without rhyme or reason had been brought to life by a spider?

It took me a while to respond and, when I did, it wasn't much of a response at all. "What?"

"A spider! TherewasaspideronmeSteven! I woke up andtherewasaspideronme!"

She was babbling. She swung at my chest again. When the punch missed, she kicked me in the shin. She'd transformed from Usain Bolt to Anderson Silva, and I wasn't particularly interested in making out with either one.

I tried to calm her down. I went back into the bedroom and pretended that I killed all the "spiders" I couldn't find. I tried my damndest to coax her back into bed. I would have told her that Ryan Gosling was nude under the cover and primed for action, if it would have gotten her to calm down and go back to sleep.

She wasn't having it.

I offered to sleep on the couch with her, safely tucked away from the bedroom and what were apparently the world's deadliest spiders in the history of spiders.

She still wasn't listening.

My wife was gone. The woman I'd married nearly thirteen years prior had checked out. The insane bundle of twitchy nerves and incomprehensible gibberish shivering before me was all that remained.

Here's the deal: A month prior to the "Great Spider Armageddon of 2012," my wife had won a week's stay at a cabin in the mountains an hour or so away from our house. At first, she was excited. For years she'd been complaining *cough* bitching *cough*cough* about the fact she want to "get in touch with nature," again.

I tried to explain to her that nature sucks. I really did. Nature is a jerk. Real life birds are annoying, disease infested things that don't care if you want them to shut up, and they have, absolutely, no issue with dropping their feces on your head. Birds on my television can go away the instant I want them to go away and, only occasionally, does it end in a feceshat. Nature is annoying.

I tried to talk her out of nature, and I tried to talk her out of a trip to the mountains, but she wasn't listening.

As much as I wanted to say, *"I told you so"* while watching her sob in the corner, fearful of the next spider onslaught, I held my tongue. I had more pressing matters to deal with.

At that point, there were only two options available: deal with her craziness until the sun came up or drive down the side of a mountain in the middle of the night to take her home.

She suddenly jumped onto the couch, clawing at her legs and knocking over a table in the center of the room. "One of them is on me! Ohgodoneofthemisonme! Do something, Steven! Dosomethingdosomethingdosomethingdosomething!"

I grabbed my keys.

The road was dark. There aren't any streetlights on the side of a mountain. The streets twisted and turned, and for most of the trip I had little to no idea where I was or where I was going. One wrong turn, one misplaced turn of the wheel and we would have ended up in a pile of twisted metal at the bottom of a ravine.

It was stupid. And it was all because of a spider.

I told you so, hun.

SUPER SHITSHINS TO THE RESCUE

SUPER SHITSHINS TO THE RESCUE

"Your reign on top was short, like leprechauns. As I crush so-called willies, thugs, and rapper-dons."

Damn straight, Biggie.

Don't get me wrong, those lyrics are a wee bit silly, but damn straight, Biggie.

That's what I was listening to.

That's what I was listening to the day I nearly died.

I'm not sure what that says about me. *Probably nothing at all.*

White dudes in their thirties who enjoy an occasional track from the late Mr. Smalls are the coolest white dudes of all, right?

No?

In any case, it was a night like any other night. The sun had long since set, and I was enjoying/hating every moment of my nightly jog/run. The rhymes of a rather plump African American rapper were pumping through my ears, tickling my brain with thier lispy lyrical goodness. My shins were hurting because my shins always hurt when I run/walk.

They're shitshins.

That's what shitshins do.

I was in pain, serious pain. My shins were throbbing like the babyhole of a cat in heat. They were hurting more then Will Smith's ego after *Wild Wild West*. I needed to take a break. I also needed to catch my breath, but I'm going to blame it on my deficient shins rather than my piss-poor athleticism.

Less than five seconds after stopping, inhaling, and trying to ignore the sound of my lower legs cracking, something flew past me. It was huge. Three thousand pounds of steel and gas, and gears, and hoses, and rubber, and leather and whatever else is used to make a a car leap off of the road behind me and took to the air. It flipped onto the sidewalk, steel screaming, glass flying. It smashed through a tree and a row of bushes, spinning and tossing dirt in every direction. When it finally stopped, it was just ten feet away, headlights shattered, driver side collapsed, smoke seeping from underneath the twisted hood.

Holy shit.

Holy shit. Shit.

Sholy Hit.

I didn't move, didn't even blink.

Amazingly, I hadn't crapped my pants.

Suddenly, I was moving forward. I didn't particularly want to move forward, but that's exactly what I was doing. I couldn't tell if anyone was alive inside the flying deathtrap that nearly transformed me into a racing stripe on the underpants of a poorly wiped backside. I couldn't image how anyone would be.

Seemed impossible.

I was fully expecting to see something that resembled the crisper tray in Jeffery Dahmer's refrigerator when I arrived at what was left of the passenger side door – a literal *head* of lettuce, pinky fingers instead of baby carrots, a scooped out skull being used as a guacamole serving dish.

It was going to be gross. I just knew it was going to be gross. It had to be gross.

Amazingly, the passenger side window was intact. At first glance, I didn't see any severed limbs.

So that was a good thing.

While the door was a complete mess, the window seemed to be hanging in there. I leaned in close. I could vaguely make out the shadow of a person in the driver's seat. It was moving. It was a woman. Her head seemed to be exactly where her head was supposed to be. Her arms looked attached, fingers still in place.

"Are you okay?"

She didn't respond.

"Are you hurt?"

"Went from ten G's for blow to thirty G's a show, to orgies with hoes I never seen befo."

Damn it, I still had my earbuds in. *That would have been a really odd response from her.*

I popped them out. "Can you move?"

"I'm okay. I don't…I don't know…"

She was shaken up. She was babbling, not making much sense. A light near the hood caught my eye, the warm glimmer of fire. Something was on fire under the car.

While I don't know a hell of a lot about cars – *nothing actually* - I knew enough to realize that fire probably wasn't supposed to be there. It probably wasn't flaming like Bruce Vilanch at Harvey Fierstein's sixty-third birthday bash when they drove it off the assembly line.

"You should probably get out, if you can." I tried to open the passenger side door. Unfortunately it looked like Rihanna's face after a romantic afternoon with her *man*. It wouldn't budge.

I had to do something.

"Get back."

The passenger side window was open just a smidge at the top. I wedged my fingers inside, held tight and pulled toward me. The glass shattered a hell of a lot easier than I thought it would.

Leaning into the window, I wrapped my arms around the girl, pulled her from the car, moved her away from the wreck and sat her down on a rock. By this time, a bunch of cars had stopped and a small crowd had gathered. There were police sirens in the distance, maybe a fire truck. Some guy hopped from his SUV, knelt beside the girl and started asking her questions. Other people were talking on their cell phones. A few more were using those very same phones to snap candid shots of the flaming car. Shadowgirl seemed shaken. Her hair was a mess, eyes glassy. She also seemed a little drunk.

Moron.

For the first time since her car nearly wiped me from existence, I realized that I had very nearly been wiped from existence. This broad's car nearly transformed me into a Tom Savini make-up effect. If my shitshins hadn't been performing to their absolute shittiest ability, I'd have been a goner.

That's it.

Gonezo.

The end.

Nothing left but a mashed up smudge of powdered bones and half digested pizza.

That would have been all she wrote.

The fat lady would have sung and the fat man would have died of complications due to his early-onset diabetes.

Some poor bastard would have been scraping the mushed remains of my brain off the sidewalk and picking it out of the grass for days.

I didn't want to be there, anymore.

I wanted to go home.

I returned the earbuds to my ears, tossed the hood over my head and took off like a goof ball. I think someone said something to me. I ignored them. A jog turned into a run rather quickly and a run became a full-on sprint shortly afterward. The flaming car, and the crowd of people, and the tipsy dope who nearly transformed me into me a barely-there memory in the minds of a few, disappeared into the night.

When I got home, I headed straight to the bedroom. My wife was on the phone. I told her to get off.

"Face to face, out in the heat. Hangin' tough, stayin' hugry."

Fucking earbuds.

And so what if I listen to Eye of the Tiger when I run?

When the wife didn't get off the phone, I yelled at her. "Just get off the phone!"

I spent the next ten minutes telling her what happened while pacing back and forth, unable to believe it myself. She sat silently, twiddling her fingers, never blinking and barely breathing. When I was done, she said I was like a superhero, that I might have saved that girl's life.

Yep, that's me, Shitshins McGee, shattering windows and rescuing half-drunk morons from flaming cars.

She also mentioned that I probably should have stayed there to answer any questions the police might have.

That part wasn't very superhero like.

In fact, running away like it was the end of a Benny Hill sketch was so un-superhero like that I probably shouldn't have included it in this story.

That part doesn't make me look too cool.

Oh well, why change things now?

ABOUT THE AUTHOR

Steven Novak is a writer, illustrator, graphic designer, podcaster, and lover of all things full-blown nerdy and vaguely nerd-related. He currently resides in southern California, where he lives with his wife of over ten years. Sometimes he forgets to shave and because of this he often sports a rather shaggy beard. Goats Eat Cans Volume 3 is the final installment in an ongoing series. For more information check out **goatseatcans.blogspot.com** More of his work can be found at **novakillustration.com**

www.ingramcontent.com/pod-product-compliance
Lightning Source LLC
LaVergne TN
LVHW051823080426
835512LV00018B/2697